"watch for the robin..."

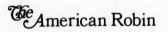

The American Robin

The American Robin

A Backyard Institution

Len Eiserer

Line Drawings by Martha R. Hall

Nelson-Hall *nh* Chicago

Library of Congress Cataloging in Publication Data

Eiserer, Len.
  The American robin.

  Includes index.
  1. Robins. I. Title.
QL696.P288E35   598.8'42   76-25438
ISBN 0-88229-228-5

Manufactured in the United States of America

To Robins everywhere, that they may continue
to prosper beyond human reckoning of time; and
to California Condors of eons now passed, that
they may forgive us what we have done.

Contents

Preface

The American Robin may well be the most familiar and best-liked bird on our continent—and not surprisingly so. In addition to sporting a distinctive plumage and boasting a wide distribution (he is probably North America's most numerous native bird), the Robin sings a spirit-lifting carol and displays before everyone a fascinating talent for catching worms. He warms winter-wearied people with welcome news of spring and then graciously accepts their hospitality by nesting on the window sills of their homes. Small wonder our Robin is perched atop the charts of avian popularity!

And yet just how much do most people really know about this redbreasted fellow? Do they know how he got his name, where he spends the night, or what happens to him if he doesn't go south for the winter? Do they understand his territorial nature, his vulnerability to pesticides, or his ecological requirements for nesting? Do they know how long a baby Robin may be expected to live? Despite the Robin's great popularity, most people know little about the details of his habits and needs. This lack of knowledge about so commonplace an animal offers a telling comment on the success of our current efforts to become educated in the complexities of both our environment and the wildlife that share it with us.

It is not that little is known about Robins in scientific circles. Indeed, the Robin has been observed and studied by a multitude of professional ornithologists and amateur birdwatchers. The resulting information, while far from complete, is nevertheless considerable. Still, a systematic synthesis of this information into a comprehensive description of the Robin's entire life cycle has not yet been made. This book is intended to remedy that situation.

Acknowledgments

No matter how many times I place a drop of pond water beneath the lens of a microscope, I am awed by the myriad of wondrous, heretofore invisible animals that suddenly materialize before my eyes. Whom should I thank for this breathtaking journey to Liliput? The animals themselves, for being what they are? Or the microscope and those who created it, for making my trip possible?

A similar quandary faced me with the dedication of this book, for the Robins portrayed herein are viewed not simply through my own eyes, but rather through a "microscope" constructed with details provided by more than a thousand ornithologists, birdwatchers, and bird lovers. Except for occasional attempts at humor and alliteration, my own contributions consist primarily of synthesis and, I hope, a few interesting insights. Most of the facts have come from others, many of whom spent weeks, months, even years observing Robins in the field. Unfortunately, a great number of these men and women are now dead. But to all of them, I—as well as every reader of this book—owe a debt that cannot be repaid.

A second note of thanks goes to my mate, Patricia Anne Lemay, affectionately known as Pretty Pumpernickel, for her invaluable criticisms and suggestions, for her help in many phases of the library work, and above all for her genuine understanding of what this book has meant to me. I'd have dedicated this book to her, if only she were a Robin.

chapter 1

Hey! Wasn't That a Robin?

> Sometimes birds are misidentified because of tricky lighting effects that are ever present in Nature. It is always with a chuckle that I recall a bird that Robert P. Allen and I saw dash into a large bush on a New Jersey salt marsh only a few years ago. With our glasses we noticed that it had a green back and stripes on the throat. "A European species," we whispered to each other, "or at least one from the Northwest." It was a shy migrant and it did not feel safe on a salt marsh. After a full five minutes we finally saw it well. It was a Robin.
>
> —Joseph J. Hickey, 1943

Is there anyone in the United States or Canada who—barring illusions of the sort that fooled Hickey and Allen—does not recognize the American Robin at a glance? Even the most casual observer of birds knows the male Robin to be about ten inches in stature, with a dark brown back, an even darker head, a yellow bill, perhaps some white on his tail and vent, and of course the trademarkish red breast. His mate is not much different, except that her head and back may be a little lighter, her breast a bit duller.

Yet a traveler visiting all corners of the continent would soon discover that not all Robins look exactly alike. Ornithologists have classified six or seven different populations of Robins that vary among themselves in either size or shading or both. To be sure, the differences that separate these subspecies, or races, may appear rather trivial to the eyes of a layman; in fact, even the ornithologists themselves are not unanimous on the validity of distinguishing a few of the groups. (For example, it's debatable whether Robins living in parts of Mexico are a separate population from United States races.) And while the geographical ranges of the half-dozen recognized races tend to be mutually distinct, there is considerable overlap in several cases.

Robin Races

In any event, the most widely accepted populations of Robins include:

1. *The Eastern Robin,* who breeds throughout eastern North America and, despite his name, as far northwest as Alaska. This bird, some ten inches in length, is the "typical" Robin to which the other races are usually compared.

2. *The Southern Robin,* who breeds from Illinois and Maryland south to northern Mississippi, Alabama, and South Carolina. This race is smaller than the Eastern Robin, and its colors (for example, on the breast) are paler.

3. *The Black-Backed Robin* breeds in northeastern Quebec, Labrador, Newfoundland, and New Brunswick. This race is a bit larger than the Eastern Robin and also much darker throughout, with (as its name suggests) a blacker back.

4. *The Western Robin* breeds from British Columbia to Mexico and from the Pacific Ocean to the Great Plains. This race, slightly larger than the Eastern Robin, is similar in color except that the outer tail feathers lack white tips, the back is a bit lighter, and the breast somewhat paler.

5. *The Northwestern Robin* breeds from Alaska south through the Pacific Coast region of British Columbia into northwestern Washington. This race is about the same size as the Eastern Robin (and thus is smaller than the Western Robin), but lacks the extended white on the tail feathers. In shading, the Northwestern Robin is much darker than the Western Robin and perhaps a little darker than the Eastern Robin.

6. *The San Lucas Robin* is classified as a distinct species, and breeds in Lower California around the Cape region. This beautiful Robin is quite pale, with a cream-colored breast and gray instead of black on his head.

It must be emphasized that none of these groups is really much different from any of the others. An occasional Western Robin may actually be as dark as the typical Northwestern Robin. Or the light-colored female of one race (for example, the Eastern) may closely resemble the male of another race (for example, the Southern). Or there may even be intermediate forms of Robin occurring between two given populations.

Inasmuch as the breeding grounds of one subspecies may be the winter resort of a more northerly group, representatives of two different races may find themselves hunting side by side on the same lawn or football field during the hectic migration season. If so, then the two races inevitably intermix without restraint, totally ignoring the subtle differences between them in unhuman-like fashion. A Robin is, after all, a Robin, and no degree of mere racial distinction can ever change that reality.

Albinism and Melanism

A description of the Robin's plumage would not be complete without noting occasionally occurring exceptions to typical Robin coloration. Albinism constitutes one of these exceptions. While never frequent, cases of albinism appear to be less rare among Robins than among most other species of bird (albinos are also relatively common among English Sparrows, Redwinged Blackbirds, and Cliff Swallows).·

Among Robins, albino individuals can be grouped into three categories that differ in the degree to which whiteness dominates the body's coloration. *Partial albinos* have several or many white feathers within their plumage, leading to a somewhat "streaky" appearance. Usually the head is normally pigmented, but white feathers are intermixed with normal feathers on the wings, tail, breast, or back, or on any combination of these areas. More often than not the white streaks present an asymmetrical pattern. *White Robins* are extreme examples of partial albinism, since they are completely white all over. However, they differ from *total albinos* by having the Robin's typical dark brown eyes. A total albino has eyes which lack pigmentation and appear pink because of blood vessels in the eyes themselves.

This absence of eye shadow in total albinos, by the way, can make for a neat trick the next time such a Robin walks up to you. Beam a bright light into one of the Robin's eyes while you look into the other. You'll find that the eyeball you're eyeing shines quite like a glowing furnace, as if the creature's head were filled with coal instead of brain. This bird-beacon effect is possible because a Robin's eyes are nearly opposite each other and because only translucent cartilage separates the two oculi once light gets by the pigmentless peepers.

Albinistic Robins almost surely have a shorter average life span than do normal Robins. First and foremost, albinos are robbed of their protective coloration and in fact are made downright conspicuous before the ever-searching eyes of predators. Another factor working against an albino—or at least a total albino—is decreased visual ability, since the bird's unpigmented eyes may have trouble functioning up to par in bright sunlight. Still a third disadvantage is the fact that albinos often possess a weaker constitution in general than normal birds, and thus they may not be as resistant to disease and harsh weather. Despite all these problems, however, exceptional longevity is sometimes achieved by an albino Robin; one male whose body was nearly all white was seen in Norristown, Pennsylvania, from 1939 to 1947, a span of nine years. Few normally colored Redbreasts manage to live that long!

What effect, if any, white plumage has on a Robin's social life has yet to be satisfactorily determined. A few observers have reported isolated incidents of cruel ostracism on the part of other Robins toward their blanched fellow. But on the whole, albinos— whether partial or total—appear to be accepted members of Robin society. They are welcome at the flock's communal feeding grounds and, if they live long enough, they are often able to secure a breeding partner. This latter fact may explain why albinism is not as rare among Robins as among other birds; perhaps albinos in other species are not acceptable as mates and thus are denied the opportunity to pass on their albino trait to the next generation. Interestingly enough, it appears that female albino Robins are more successful in finding mates than male albino Robins are.

Another type of exceptional coloration is melanism, where the plumage is very dark or actually black. This abnormality is much rarer in Robins than albinism, and melanistic specimens are highly valued by persons who obtain them. One black Robin was owned by a saloon keeper near Jersey City, New Jersey, way back in 1880. This enterprising gentleman at first set a fancy price for his bird and, failing to find a purchaser, finally raffled off his sooty gem at $2.00 a chance!

In many cases, both melanism and albinism are undoubtedly rooted in genetics. Although albino mothers often rear babies who have perfectly normal plumage, the chances of begetting a pale-faced youngster are much greater with an albinistic parent than if both mom and pop are pigmented normally. Indeed, total albinism is probably entirely congenital in origin.

Partial albinism, on the other hand, is at least sometimes developed through the course of an individual's lifetime. One Robin, for example, possessed normal plumage when initially banded, but was a partial albino when recovered two years later. Numerous other cases of gradual change in color have been recorded, particularly among Robins who at the time were living in captivity. Frequently these birds undergo a melanistic phase before entering an albinistic phase. Since melanism reflects an excessive increase in black pigment (which is called melanin), continuation of this condition may possibly exhaust the supply of, and hinder the ability to renew, melanin; if so, then albinism might be expected to ensue.

But just exactly what physiological perturbation ultimately underlies such chameleonic changes is unclear. One ornithologist of the last century suggested that partial albinism was due to tapeworms in the intestine, since he had frequently discovered those creatures in albino Robins as well as in albinistic individuals of other species. Conceivably these parasites could extract and monopolize some important color ingredient from the host's diet. Although most of the reported caged Robins appear to have received well-balanced meals, subtle dietary deficiencies may nevertheless have been an important factor. It's been found, for example, that large mineral deficiencies often exist in the bones of abnormally colored Robins. Also, captive flamingos who have paled usually get back in the pink after eating shrimp!

Other Physical Abnormalities

Rare color of plumage, of course, is not the only manner in which Robins can express their nonconformity. Sometimes the abnormalities are hidden from casual human observation, as in the case of a dead female who, upon being dissected, was found to possess only one lung, the left lung being entirely missing. Other times the deformities are blatant, sacrilegious affronts to the Robin's normally good looks. In 1965, for example, two different baby Robins (one in New York, the other in West Virginia) were found with their respective tongues protruding down through their lower mandibles. In both instances the plight was probably the result of abnormal development rather than accidental injury. Misguided development also occasionally leads to eyeless babies who may survive well enough while under the solicitous care of their parents but who are otherwise doomed to a premature end.

Other deformities may not be fatal but merely nuisances or, perhaps even worse, embarrassments. One Robin completely lacked a tail and yet managed to return to his territory in the Boston Public Garden during three successive springs, thereby demonstrating that you don't need a rudder to navigate the long Robin migrations. Another bird, this one an adolescent hailing from Pennsylvania, grew two tails that were missing one and two feathers respectively (twelve is the normal number of tail feathers) but were otherwise typical posteriors of the species.

As with tails, legs are a commodity in short supply for some Robins and a bit too abundant for others. One-legged Robins have frequently been reported, many no doubt the products of accidents though some may have been defective since birth. With a little practice these hop-a-long birds manage surprisingly well, although landing on a perch may present ever-recurring difficulties. Perhaps the strangest Robin of all, however, was a youngster who had three normal legs. Two of these limbs were on the left side, one above the other, while the third was in its regular position on the right.

Before we leave the physical characteristics of the American Robin, idle interest inspires mention of a few other facts. Adults usually weigh from seventy to eighty grams (about six birds to the pound), although their weights change a bit before and after migration and, in females, during the reproductive season. Nearly 15 percent of this weight is contributed by the Robin's flight muscles, and only 4 percent by the bird's hollow skeleton. When the Robin rests, his heart pumps some three hundred fifty times per minute, and his lungs suck and spout air about forty-five times per minute. The Robin's body holds a temperature of around 109.7°F (although this varies with activity and time of day) and is covered by approximately twenty-nine hundred feathers (compared to twenty-five thousand for swans and zero for most humans).

How Robin Got His Name

With these important facts behind us, let's see why we call that redbreasted worm-hunter who patrols your front lawn a Robin. In Normandy of long, long ago, people used to refer to a love-struck adolescent as "Robert" (a name that means "gleaming fame"), and this word was eventually abbreviated to "Robin." The Normans brought the term to the British Isles when they invaded in 1066 A.D., and the name was given to a small bird who previously had been called "ruddock" because of his red breast. This little bird, who like a fiery youth in love vigorously defended his nesting territory against all challengers, was called "robynet redbreast" (meaning "little Robin Redbreast"), or later, simply "Robin." This English or European Robin looks much like our Eastern Bluebird in both size and color, and is the fellow appearing so often in British literature (for example, he played the role of hero in the melancholy tale of "Babes in the Wood," in which he blanketed the chilled title characters with leaves).

When the English colonists came to this country and failed to find their beloved Redbreast here, they gave his name to our much larger Robin who—while bearing a similar ruddy breast, robust spirit, and friendly disposition—is actually not too closely related to the English bird at all. Comparable nostalgic christenings by homesick Britons have befallen birds in many parts of the world, birds frequently having little in common with the European Robin except a reddish breast.

Even our American Robin, however, has a few namesakes of his own. One is the Beach Robin, a redbreasted Sandpiper who winters along the eastern coast of the United States. Another is the Sea-Robin, a homely flat-nosed fish who sort of resembles a bird because of its large winglike pectoral fins, and who vaguely resembles a Robin because of its generally reddish color. Sea-Robins are common along the eastern coast as far north as Cape Cod.

We might also mention that our Redbreast has other names besides American Robin. A common one is "Fieldfare," which is another hand-me-down label from a British bird, this one a migratory thrush of the same name. French Canadians used to refer to our Robin as "Merle," and the Pennsylvania Dutch called him "Omshel." And of course our native Americans, the Indians, had their own names for the Robin: the Dog-rib Indians near Great Slave Lake in northwestern Canada called him "Goshi," while the northeastern Penobscots referred to him as "Cha La Cha Lee."

In addition to having all of these common or popular labels, the Robin travels in the world of biologists under a latinized alias which constitutes the bird's scientific name. Every known living creature, both plant and animal, has been classified by taxonomists along a hierarchy of increasingly specific groupings. This classification system, founded by the great Swedish botanist Karl Linnaeus during the eighteenth century, assigns for each plant and animal its own little identification tag so that scientists won't lose it within the enormous variety of Nature. The Robin's tag reads as follows:

KINGDOM: *Animalia* (as opposed to plants)

PHYLUM: *Chordata* (animals with a notochord or backbone)

CLASS:	*Aves* (chordates who are birds)
ORDER:	*Passeriformes* (perching birds, as opposed to, say, Penguins)
FAMILY:	*Turdidae* (perching birds who are thrushes)
GENUS:	*Turdus* (one of five different thrush genera)
SPECIES:	*migratorius* (all American Robins except the San Lucas Robin, whose species is *confinis*)

For most purposes it is sufficient to identify an animal only in terms of genus and species. Thus the Robin is known in the inner circles as simply *Turdus migratorius*, which in Latin means "wandering thrush" (a perfectly appropriate name, as we shall later see). If one wants to further specify a particular race of Robins, an additional term must be cited: *Turdus migratorius migratorius* (Eastern Robin), *Turdus migratorius achrusterus* (Southern Robin), *Turdus migratorius nigrideus* (Black-Backed Robin), *Turdus migratorius propinquus* (Western Robin), *Turdus migratorius caurinus* (Northwestern Robin), and *Turdus migratorius permixtus* or *phillipsi* for two of the questionable Mexican races of American Robin.

It is important to realize that the particular groups to which an animal belongs are not chosen by scientists arbitrarily but instead represent an attempt to delineate the evolutionary relationships that a given species bears to other living things. For example, by knowing that the European Blackbird's Latin name is *Turdus merula*, one can deduce that scientists believe this bird to be more closely related to our Robin (since both birds are grouped within the same genus—*Turdus*) than either bird is related to the Common Crow *(Corvus brachyrhynchos)* or to the European Robin *(Erithacus rubecula)*. To a large extent, this relationship is reflected in physical similarities between the two species. As true thrushes, both the Robin and Blackbird lay bluish-green eggs, tend to have slender bills, and have speckled breasts (in the young of the Robin, in the female of the Blackbird).

But in addition to physical resemblances, evolutionary relationships are also reflected within the dimension of behavior. Indeed, the American Robin and European Blackbird probably resemble each other more in terms of their behavior than they do physically—they both use mud in building their nests, they both rear more than one brood each season, their songs are rather similar, and they practice similar lawn-running habits.

Fortunately, the early English colonists failed to notice this close behavioral similarity of our Robin to their Blackbird and instead saw only the superficial similarity of color with their own tiny Robin. Otherwise we might all be singing, "When the red, red Blackbird goes bob-bob-bobbin' along." And that just doesn't rhyme.

chapter 2

A Story of Species Success

"Relicts" are species that tend to become more and more restricted both geographically and ecologically, because they are unable to compete successfully with other species. At the other extreme are those dominant or ultra-successful species that are expanding geographically and also, in many cases, in ecological tolerance. The American Robin *(Turdus migratorius)* is an example.

—Dean Amadon, 1953

Without a doubt, Robins are much more widespread and numerous today than they were five hundred years ago. Robins thus tell a story of species success that has seldom been attained in the animal kingdom, at least within the past couple millennia. To be sure, a few other organisms have also achieved great and recent success; humans and rats, for instance, can both boast representatives almost planetwide. But when considered against the countless species that are having difficulty holding their own in today's world, the countless others that are quickly becoming extinct, and the still countless others that have already passed out of existence, the American Robin is surely among the biological elite. Indeed—forgetting for the moment the indestructible insects, the ubiquitous microorganisms, and the unapproachable fish of the sea—Mother Earth may one day look at herself and, despite a most thorough search, find little more than Robins, rats, and people scurrying about her surface.

Robin Haunts

Robins can be found in quite a wide variety of environments, including mountains and valleys, forests and seashores, cities and farms; at times they even visit deserts and the treeless arctic tundra. The Robin's preferred breeding habitat, however, contains open, grassy ground for feeding, and sturdy, low-limbed trees for nesting and shelter. Modern suburban areas, with their fine-trimmed lawns and scattered orchard and shade trees, are thus ideal breeding forums for Redbreasts.

Interestingly, the large stretches of heavily cluttered forest that covered much of pre-colonial America did not provide a very conducive habitat for the ground-feeding Robin. Instead, the birds probably gathered most densely around sporadically occurring forest clearings or near forest edges (that is, the borders between woods and open fields). Such areas were then tolerably common, at least in the northeastern part of the continent, and the Robin was accordingly a tolerably common bird—populous here and there, scarce more generally. When, however, humans axed forests to form fields and lawns, and later when they irrigated sand and sagebrush to grow trees and grass, Robins mushroomed in both range and number.

Today, Robins live across all of North America, from the Atlantic to the Pacific coast, and from the middle of Mexico to the upper regions of Canada. This impressive distribution, however, needs to be qualified in several ways. First, since Robins are a migratory species, the areas in which they breed are not necessarily identical to the areas in which they—during the different seasons—regularly appear. Although virtually no region of the continent fails to see Robins sometime during the year, the Far

North hosts few Redbreasts during the winter and, until relatively recently, the Far South saw few during the summer.

Secondly, the fact that Robins breed in a given habitat does not imply that they prosper or even hold their own there. Robins can be found in most urban areas, for example, despite mortality rates that may be twice as high as that suffered by Redbreasts living in rural areas where cats and dogs—major enemies of breeding Robins—are generally more scarce. In fact, some urban areas may retain Robin populations even though more birds die in the city than are born there! Apparently, a city's population can continue to survive under such circumstances because of regular influxes by surplus Robins from surrounding suburban areas.

A third qualifying note to the Robin's wide distribution is that the birds may be extremely numerous within a restricted area and yet be quite scarce or even absent throughout immediately surrounding regions. This island-of-Robins effect can occur in many different contexts. In frontier regions (for example, the Far North, or mountain areas), Robins may be absent except near the isolated villages that spot the area, and in these they will be common. In swamps and bogs where Redbreasts don't usually hold extended residence, flocks may congregate around small patches of berries that have suddenly ripened, while surrounding areas have no Robins at all. After a springtime snowstorm, when nearly all the ground is cloaked in white, Robins may sardine themselves onto one forageable green patch that somehow escaped the covering. And in a comparable manner, a source of water in an otherwise desert region will attract Robins in great numbers while neighboring regions are completely Robinless.

Incidentally, although Robins are inhabitants of North America almost exclusively, Redbreasts have occasionally popped up in such distant realms as Bermuda, Cuba, Greenland, Britain, Ireland, and Austria. Once, an American Robin was even sighted on Helgoland, a tiny mile-long island whose 200-foot cliffs project from the North Sea some forty miles off the mouth of Germany's River Elbe. Redbreasts have apparently never ventured to Australia, probably in deference to the giant seven-foot earthworms that tunnel through that strange continent.

Robins are quite able to reach the nearer of these foreign lands (that is, Bermuda and Cuba) under their own birdpower, but some of the European sightings probably involved individuals who were released, or who escaped, from captivity in those lands. The possibility remains, however, that a stray Robin or two has actually managed to cross the Atlantic Ocean in some spirited Lindberghian adventure. While Robins generally try to avoid flying over the open sea, they will travel over long stretches of water to reach numerous islands on which they regularly breed (for example, the Magdalen Islands, which lie off Quebec in the Gulf of St. Lawrence, sixty to seventy miles from any major land mass). There is, in addition, one report of a Redbreast who cruised by a ship that was chugging four hundred miles off the eastern coast.

Regional Variations among Robins

One interesting sidelight of the Robin's extensive distribution is the existence of various differences among groups of Redbreasts residing in different localities. A blatant behavioral dissimilarity, for example, is shown by those Robins who breed in areas where human beings are scarce (for example, near the arctic limits) and those who breed in suburban backyards. Usually the latter are relatively trusting animals who parade about in plain view of people, while the former are wild, wary, and extremely difficult to approach.

The slight color and size variations displayed by the numerous races of Redbreasts provide another illustration of group differences among Robins. As previously noted, these subspecies distinctions are generally associated with various geographic regions; nevertheless, a single region can sometimes contain two separate races, with each restricted to a relatively exclusive ecological niche. As we shall see shortly, there are areas of the southern United States where Eastern Robins inhabit the mountains while Southern Robins live throughout the surrounding lowlands. Another example has, at least in the past, characterized the Washington-Oregon area where both the Western and the Northwestern Robin have been found to breed. Again, the two races prefer slightly different habitats, for while the Western Robin has lived primarily within human-inhabited districts, the Northwestern Robin has instead resided in nearby tracts of coniferous forest.

Numerous reproductive variations exist within the Robin population. First, due to the obvious differences in the schedule of spring's arrival, the early-nesting southern populations enjoy a much longer breeding season than the later-nesting northern groups; as a result, the former can frequently rear three broods in a single season while the latter, especially in the Far North, may manage only one. There also seems to be a tendency for the offspring of Robins in the Far North (for example, at Umiat, which is at an arctic latitude of 69°N) to leave their nests a few days sooner than the offspring of Robins living in the United States.

A third reproductive variation is in nest-building materials: grass and mud are the most general ingredients to a Robin's nest, but Redbreasts in northern Maine may instead use twigs and leaf-mold while birds even farther north may build with moss and lichen. Even clutch-size (the number of eggs laid) varies with place of residence, for Robins tend to lay slightly smaller clutches at lower latitudes (two or three eggs at Mexico City's 20°N latitude) than at higher ones (three to five eggs in the northern United States). Interestingly, clutches also tend to become somewhat smaller with increasing nearness to the coastline, at least across the northeastern part of the continent.

A final distribution-related difference exists between mountain-living Robins and lowland-living Robins; the former usually have heavier hearts and lungs than do the latter. Why? Because the mountain birds, flying as they do at such lofty altitudes, must somehow cope with respiratory and circulatory problems engendered by the mountain air's decreased density, poorer oxygen content, and lower temperature. Apparently, larger lungs and heavier hearts do the trick.

Altitude Equals Latitude

According to a basic principle of ecology, many of the differences between southern regions and northern regions—in terms of climate, vegetation, and wildlife—are paralleled by comparable differences between lowlands and mountains. In other words, the same sort of ecological changes that a person would observe in traveling from a southern latitude toward a northern latitude can also be observed as one gains altitude by climbing up a tall mountain.

Climatically, this altitude-equals-latitude principle is reflected in the dropping of both temperature and air pressure as one approaches either the arctic (from the south) or a mountain peak (from the lowlands). Vegetationwise, the same succession of plant life that occurs as one moves from the equator to the arctic—namely, from tropical forest to deciduous forest, to coniferous forest, to mosses and lichens, and finally to bare ice and snow—also tends to occur with increasing altitude along an equatorial mountain (the mountain would have tropical forests surrounding its base, coniferous forests halfway up, and unvegetated ice and snow at its peak). Even the changes occurring in animal life across increasing latitudes can find parallels in the species living at progressively increasing heights along a moun-

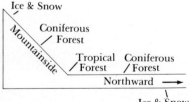

tain slope; thus fur tends to thicken (for better insulation), tails and ears tend to shorten (to minimize loss of body heat by decreasing the body's surface area), and gestation periods tend to increase (so that babies are more developed at birth, and therefore better able to face harsh arctic or mountaintop climates).

Robins follow this altitude-equals-latitude principle in quite a number of different ways. First, while the majority of Redbreasts use twigs, grass, and mud to make their nests, both mountain-dwelling Robins and Robins of the Canadian north frequently use lichen and moss as major nest materials. A second example involves molting (changing of plumage), for both mountain Robins and northern Robins tend to molt as much as a month later than do birds of the lowlands and birds of the South. Thus, in terms of both nesting materials and time of molting, those Robins who live at high altitudes show marked similarity to those Robins who live at high latitudes.

Another demonstration of the seeming equivalency of altitude and latitude is provided by the distribution of the Eastern Robin who, in parts of Virginia, the Carolinas and even Georgia, infringes upon what is normally the domain of the Southern Robin. Frequently, Eastern Robins can be found living high in the mountains while their southern relatives reside in the surrounding lowlands. The high altitudes of the South, the Eastern Robin seems to be telling us, are just as ecologically satisfactory as the high latitudes of the North.

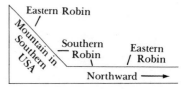

A final illustration involves *vertical migration,* which is the descent of mountain-breeding animals into nearby lowlands for the winter (vertical migration thus substitutes a decrease in altitude for a decrease in latitude as a way to circumvent winter's severity). The best example of vertical migration among Redbreasts is provided by the San Lucas Robin. Unlike most of his relatives, this beautiful but little-known member of the Robin family is strictly nonmigratory—at least in the traditional sense.

Rather than journeying southward like most Redbreasts, the San Lucas Robin simply descends from breeding grounds in the mountains of Lower California and winters in surrounding lowlands. Similar vertical migrations are performed by some of the Robins living in Mexico (of subspecies *phillipsi*), as well as some of the Robins breeding in the mountainous pine-belt regions of Washington.

These vertical migrations, incidentally, are similar to the more conventional *north-south migrations* in several ways. After arriving at their northern breeding grounds in the spring, for example, normally migrating Robins typically remain in flocks for a few days before dispersing to claim individual nesting areas. Comparable behavior is shown by mountain-breeding Robins, who also remain in flocks for a short time upon first returning to their alpine abodes. Another similarity involves the fact that northern breeding Robins usually begin nesting several weeks later than do more southern breeding individuals; in like manner, mountain-breeding Robins usually start nesting long after those Redbreasts breeding in the surrounding lowlands. In short, Robins who make vertical migrations seem to behave fundamentally the same as those who make latitudinal migrations.

Recent Expansions of Range

As of 1890, the only Robins who ever visited Fort Reno, Oklahoma, were a few migrating transients en route to someplace else. By 1924, however, Redbreasts were well settled and breeding with vigor throughout the entire district. Similar nesting invasions of areas heretofore unoccupied by *Turdus migratorius* have occurred time and again in North America. And almost always, these extensions of the species' distribution have been the direct result of human modification of the environment.

Of course, acts of Nature do occasionally extend the Robin's range. Redbreasts, for example, frequently pour into the wake of lightning-sparked forest fires where denuded soil and charred logs readily yield an abundance of worms and insects. More long-termed effects have apparently been occurring as a result of recent climatic changes; more specifically, there has in past decades been a slight trend toward increasing winter mildness within the continent's higher latitudes, and this seems to be encouraging a gradual, northward extension in the Robin's winter distribution.

Nevertheless, natural forces have generally been less striking than human activities in their effects upon the Robin's range. As noted earlier, the suburban setting—now so widespread across North America—has provided a nearly optimum breeding environment for Redbreasts. Indeed, Robins today are probably far more populous in these "artificial" habitats than anywhere else. Let us now, however, consider additional and more specific cases of human-wrought ecological changes that have proved beneficial to the Robin species.

One rather localized example was recently provided by a certain forest in Pennsylvania which, in its natural state of heavy underbrush, originally hosted few Robins (less than five pairs per hundred acres). Most of the undergrowth was eventually cleared away in a campsite-making project, however, and before long Robins had increased to an average density of fourteen pairs per hundred acres—a climb of more than 180 percent within a couple of years! Another quick increase in Robins occurred during World War II near Churchill, Manitoba, an area which until then was largely uncivilized wilderness. However, construction of an airport as well as several other war-inspired building projects brought great changes to the environment—changes of which Robins evidently approved, for the birds were soon several times more numerous in Churchill than ever before.

On a grander scale, Robins have succeeded in colonizing whole continental regions—specifically, the midwestern, western, and southern parts of the United States—where they were previously absent or scarce during the breeding season, if not year-round. The midwestern invasion centered upon the Great Plains where, historically, Robins had been discouraged from foraging by the tall grasses, and from nesting by the virtual absence of trees. As told by one author:

> Before the prairies of the Middle West were settled, and when bison roamed in vast herds over the boundless grassy plains, Robins bred only in the northern woods of Michigan, Wisconsin, and Minnesota. But, as civilization moved westward and trees were planted about the ranches, the Robins adapted themselves to the new and welcome conditions and made their summer homes near human dwellings in regions they had formerly passed over on migrations. (Tyler, 1949)

Incidentally, the gardens that settlers dug around their homes were perhaps as important as the trees they planted. The tough dirt of the plains, it seems, was initially quite wormless; when people imported potted plants for their newly tilled gardens, however, earthworms were inadvertently introduced into the region's soil. Before long, the prolific annelids were burrowing wherever gardens and lawns were cultivated, much to the Robin's dietary delight.

The spread of Robins in the Far West was perhaps typified by the invasion of southern California that occurred from about 1915 to 1925. Prior to that time, Robins nested only in northern regions of the state where persistent fog-belts and trickling mountain streams watered significant stretches of forageable, short-grassed meadows throughout the breeding season. In contrast, the dry lowlands of southern California simply did not provide Robins with sufficient food for raising their families. Some of these regions—little more than wind-tossed sand and sagebrush—were completely barren of worms as well as most insects. And even those areas that managed to support grass remained so parched under the scorching sun that earthworms summered in the deep, cool underground (where Robins couldn't reach them), while most insects persisted in their hard-bodied adult stages (rather than in their soft-bodied larval stages) and were thus much less vulnerable to predation as well as to desiccation.

But then humans grew grass to grasp the sand, sowed saplings and shrubbery to stop the wind, and whooshed in water to wet the lawns. As a result, earthworms tunneled to the top, insects languished in larval life, and Robins nurtured numerous nestlings. This instance of range extension, by the way, clearly illustrates that the Robin's pre-colonial distribution was restricted largely by requirements of food supply and, to a lesser extent, of nesting facilities; temperature *per se* was not a restraining force for the population. Of course, this is not to say that Robins have no inherent limitations regarding temperature, but simply that Redbreasts have always been able to tolerate the great thermo-variations found across present-day North America.

The most recent example of Robin expansion into a major continental region was the species' colonization of the Far South. Robins have always spent their winters in southern locales but until relatively recently never remained for the breeding season. Early southern rural areas did not provide conducive habitat for Robins inasmuch as most of the land was covered by cotton and corn crops, tall grass, and heavily undergrown forests; even the farmhouses and small towns did not have much in the way of lawns or nestworthy shrubbery. The larger cities, on the other hand, had both lawns and shade trees, and it was in these areas that breeding Robins first appeared.

Two aspects of the Robin's southern expansion deserve special note. First, in reaching the widely scattered big cities, Robins initially bypassed large stretches of unsuitable rural areas.

It was only after becoming safely entrenched in urban centers that the birds began to filter into the less desirable outlying districts. Secondly, suitable big-city environments had existed in the South several decades before Robins actually arrived (presumably, it was a sudden surplus of Redbreasts in areas farther north that had finally spurred the southern campaign). Having begun their invasion, however, Robins conquered the region relatively quickly; for example, even though Robins did not reach the northern border of Georgia until after the turn of this century, Redbreasts were nesting just above Florida (at Waycross) by 1937.

As a final example of the effects of human actions upon the Robin's distribution, let us consider the introduction of grazing cattle into a forested area which, because of heavy underbrush, has previously been an unsatisfactory environment for Redbreasts. Such a situation has occurred in many regions of North America, and is particularly interesting because it involves a continuously changing habitat that is suitable to Robins only during its middle stages. More specifically, the ensuing ecological succession typically occurs as follows:

The most immediate effect of the grazing is to clear out the underbrush—most importantly of all, the seedling trees. Then over the years, as the larger trees die but are not replaced, the forest canopy begins to yawn in this place and that, and short-grassed clearings begin to emerge. Each of these clearings, of course, is an attractive breeding area for Robins, and the birds soon move in. Next, as further grazing continues to prevent tree replacement, the forest shrinks more and more until eventually the trees form mere islands while the clearings become the sea. Nevertheless, the area probably still offers sufficient nest-sites for Robins, and so the birds remain. Finally, however, the few surviving woodland patches die out, and the Redbreasts accordingly abandon the region for more arboreal pastures. All of these changes, of course, happen only very slowly over many, many years.

One obvious question raised by all of the above examples of range extension is, where did the initial, pioneer breeders come from in the first place? In general, there seem to be at least three different possibilities, each of which has apparently occurred in one invasion or another. First, the pioneers might have been birds who had regularly wintered in the frontier region but, until the year of the invasion, had always deserted it at the first sign of spring. Alternatively, the pioneers could have been migrants who—while traveling to breeding grounds farther north—were enticed out of their flocks by an attractive and as-yet unclaimed new region. The third possibility is that the pioneers were birds who had been crowded out of their traditional breeding grounds by a local superabundancy of Robins, and had subsequently wandered into virgin territory.

In any event, we might in closing emphasize that the Robin's many successes in extending its range over pre-colonial times offer a marked contrast to the achievements of most other native North American populations. Consider, for example, the Indian. With the coming of white civilization, both the American Robin and the American Indian watched the wholesale loss of a great primeval life way. But it might be suggested (albeit with oversimplification) that while one group compromised, adapted, and consequently prospered, the other group resisted, clung to the old, and was largely destroyed.

chapter 3

The Odyssean Voyage

> Why Robbie decided to stay and live with friendly humans is a case of conjecture. He has always been free to leave, as most birds do, but he chose to adopt this family and the comforts of good food and human servants. In any case, he has never had to fly, like other Robins, to winter in Brazil.
>
> —A. Gordon Melvin, 1962

The spring migration of Robins can be a mammoth trip. Indeed, birds who have wintered in the southernmost parts of the United States may fly to Canadian regions thirty-five hundred miles away in order to breed. Thus, while not quite of Brazilian origins as Melvin mistakenly supposed, the northward trek of Redbreasts is Odyssean nevertheless.

Robins are not, of course, the only creatures who undertake these long annual trips. Countless other birds as well as numerous fish (such as eels and salmon), mammals (for example, bats and lemmings), and even insects (such as Monarch butterflies) boast comparable travels. Although the mysteries of migration have not been completely unraveled for any of these animals, diligent research has managed to answer a few questions—or at least supply a few guesses—about migratory mechanisms. In many avian species, for example, the daily lengthening of daylight that occurs as spring approaches seems to act as an alarm clock that awakens the birds from southern siestas and instills a northbound urge. Changing daylight does not appear to be so important for Robins, however, as they are instead governed primarily by trends of temperature. Thus Redbreasts, who typically appear at northern regions as soon as local temperatures hit 34°F to 36°F, move up the continent step in step with the latitudinal progression of springtime thaw.

Regardless of whether the complex machinery of Robin migration is understood well or poorly, the event is nonetheless filled with inevitable drama, for it marks the first step in the great annual renewal of the species. As they journey over hazard and hardship to northern breeding grounds, Robins are not merely retracing the fallen footsteps of the previous autumn. They are keeping an appointment with destiny—an appointment they dare not break.

General Migratory Characteristics

We might start off by noting some simple facts about Robin migration, such as air speed, the time of day chosen for flying, typical flocking patterns, and the basic flyways that are followed. Concerning speed, Robins maintain a fairly steady if unspectacular rate of 20 to 30 mph, flapping their wings about three or four times per second in the meanwhile. Neither statistic deserves much awe since other birds can fly and flap faster (for example, 50 mph for both Hummingbirds and Eagles, and five flaps per second for Goldfinches).

Though plebeian in speed, Robins are more elite in their choice of flight time. Most birds, it seems, prefer to migrate at night, for then they can feed and rest in concealed areas during daytime leisure. Nocturnal navigation, moreover, nicely circumvents predatory threats posed by the diurnal Hawks and Eagles.

Yet Robins—who migrate primarily during the day—not only find food quickly enough to afford brief refueling stops along the way, but also seem to boldly ignore the great birds of prey as well. Daytime migration, incidentally, is not without its advantages. For one, Robins are not usually among the thousands of migrant casualties who crash into the innumerable television towers that rear up in nocturnal darkness across the land.

Although migrating Robins occasionally compress into globular corks that bob along with every ripple of wind, the birds more typically form loose aggregates of individuals who are rather evenly spaced as if uniformly wary of grave underarm offense. In such spacious array, their unending numbers sometimes stretch for scores of miles, especially at the beginnings of their northward trip. One such flock took fully three February days to pass one spot in Florida. Said an observer of the sight:

> They came from a southerly direction, and were continually passing, alighting, and repassing, the general movement being northward. The air was full of them, their numbers beyond estimate, reminding one of bees. (Mackay, 1897)

This migrating mass was similarly reported by watchers some ten miles away, across the flight. Thus, ten miles wide and three days long was this ribbony river of Robins.

Though there are numerous flyways that Robins follow during the course of their trip, a popular one is the Mississippi River Valley. Draining the Gulf Coast and rippling up the great twenty-four-hundred-mile channel, streams of Robins eventually branch westward across plains and Rockies by following the Missouri River, and eastward to New England along the Ohio River. In numbers that may top a billion when they first leave the South, their ranks steadily thin because "all along the way, a Robin drops off on State Street here, or Elm Street there, as a homing male spots his own backyard" (George, 1964).

Robins do not always follow rivers, however, and in fact they sometimes choose courses that are perpendicular to even the largest of nearby waterways. Often, the migrants fly parallel to the north-south ridges of mountain systems, and in general they prefer relatively forested routes to naked stretches of, for instance, prairies. Robins almost never try to cross large bodies of water (lakes, bays, and certainly the oceans), but instead endure lengthy detours in order to stay above dry land.

Other major aspects of the Robin's springtime migration include the slow progress of the trip (independent of flight speed considerations), its discontinuous nature, and the wavelike effects it engenders. The first characteristic may evoke some surprise since we probably tend to equate the Robin's renowned early arrival with a quick trip. Quite conversely is true, however, as it is earliness and slowness that go hand in hand in avian migration. Since Robins advance up the continent on the somewhat sluggish heels of spring, they cannot fly too fast without overtaking the warm front and crashing head-on with northern storms. In contrast, other birds who remain South until springtime temperatures have already arrived in the North, can migrate much faster and still encounter only mild weather throughout their trip. As an example, suppose that spring takes fifteen days to cross the New England states; migrating Robins may cover the same territory in sixteen or seventeen days, while other species coming at a later date may need only a week.

Besides being slow, Robin migration is riddled with discontinuity across individual birds as well as across geographic regions. Epitomizing individual variability is the often reported observation that some Robins temporarily fly in east-west directions or even south, despite an overall northward progression by the general population. A given bird, furthermore, may travel 200 miles in a single flight, only to spend the next day or two foraging in one area while fellow migrants pass him by. Because of these great individual differences, the migration of the Robin population as a whole—which of course represents the average of many individuals—always displays a much steadier pace than that characterizing its component members.

Several examples can be cited as representative of regional variability in migratory progression. For one, Robins near the Pacific coast usually tend to migrate faster than those in either the middle or the eastern parts of the continent. For another, Robins typically travel faster as they get farther and farther north, almost as if they were increasingly anxious to get home. Thus birds who flew a mere fifteen to thirty miles per day at the southern start of their trip may average more than a hundred as they enter Canada and head northwesterly for Alaska.

Still another element of migratory variability involves local weather conditions. Instead of simply plodding north until their breeding grounds are reached, Robins accelerate during unusually warm periods and, conversely, reverse their progress whenever temperatures drop too cold for their liking. Many a birdwatcher has been astonished to observe Robins approaching from the north rather than from the south during a March cold spell. Such influxes can be surprisingly abrupt as the wide-ranging Redbreasts employ their tremendous avian mobility to shadow the often-elusive springtime warmth.

In sum, Robin migration is a phenomenon that is extremely discontinuous in nature. The trip is thus *not* analogous to the steady creeping of the morning sun, whose rays uniformly dawn from east to west. Rather, it is akin to the rising tide which, though consisting of individual advances and recessions, gradually climbs higher and higher up the beach as each wave tends to progress a bit beyond its predecessor.

And speaking of waves, we now come to a final general characteristic of Robin migration—namely, the wavelike effect that occurs as the population rolls through a given locality.

Should, for example, a citizen of Cincinnati, Ohio, begin watching for Robins in February, she might initially see only a sprinkling of Redbreasts, these representing the eager-beavers of the species. Somewhat later would come the "crest" of the wave as hundreds and thousands of birds—constituting the bulk of the migration—spill into the city over the span of a few days. As most of the migrants move on, however, the wave would finally spend itself until only a few splatterings of Robins remain. These latter individuals would be the city's summer residents, those birds who will breed within the unnatural urban environment along with countless other Cincinnatians.

Similar Robin waves can also be observed by simply driving one's car southward during early March. One man who did this saw no Robins as he left Minnesota, but then

> recorded an occasional Robin in northern Iowa, great numbers through central and southern Iowa, and a steady decrease in numbers through northern Missouri, until in central Missouri there were only scattered individuals—presumably the birds that were to become summer residents there. (Pettingill, 1970)

This wave, slowly rumbling up the North American landscape, was estimated to be some two hundred twenty-five miles in breadth—a veritable surfer's dream.

Sure Signs of Spring?

Each March, northern newspapers eagerly report the first sightings of Robins in nearby locales. Old Man Winter, after all, can be a depressing sort of fellow, and most people are happy to read about his demise. How many of us, upon spying our first Robin of the season, have experienced an emotional uplifting similar to that conveyed in the following passage:

> When they come back, what good cheer they bring with them! I remember one long winter spent in the

country when it seemed that spring would never come. At last one day the call of a Robin rang out, and on one of the few bare spots made by the melting snow there stood the first redbreast! It was a sight I can never forget, for the intense delight of such moments makes bright spots in a lifetime. (Merriam, 1898)

But do Robins really serve as accurate gauges of spring's arrival? Partly no, and partly yes. Partly no because not all Robins migrate south for the winter; some remain in the North. Thus it is perfectly possible to see a nonmigrating holdover as your "first Robin" when Mr. Winter is still in his prime. And partly yes because the large majority of Robins do in fact fly south for the winter, and then promptly reappear in the North with the return of warm weather. These latter birds, then, are reasonably legitimate springtime harbingers.

How, as March approaches, can you tell whether that Robin on your lawn is a genuine migrant or merely a mimicking imposter? Two clues will guide you: First, Robins who have arrived from the South will for at least a short time remain in flocks of a dozen or more individuals. In contrast, the winter holdovers—who have had to contend with thinly scattered food supplies—are usually alone or in pairs at most (more may temporarily gather at, say, a birdfeeder). Secondly, the migrants will still be fat and fit from southern feasts, while the holdovers are haggard and scrawny from fighting freeze and famine in the North. Still, by mid-February, even a scrawny Robin is a welcome sight to most of us, and we are not apt to quibble over such technicalities as we hasten to bid winter adieu.

Another often-asked question concerning the first Robins of spring is whether the initial arrivals are simply transients en route to breeding grounds farther north, or are instead the birds who will comprise the area's resident Redbreasts during the upcoming summer. While many observers claim that local Robins appear at a given locality before more northbound migrants, just the opposite has occasionally been reported. There may in fact be little reliable difference in the respective arrival times. The two sets of birds, however, can often be readily distinguished because the local residents soon separate into individual territories and begin singing with vigor, while the transients typically remain mute and in their migratory flocks.

The Robin is, in any event, an habitually early migrant. One enterprising ornithologist kept track of springtime arrivals in southern Connecticut over a forty-year period; the average arrival date for Robins was March 10—fourth earliest of fifty different species, with Grackles, Redwing Blackbirds, and Bluebirds only a day or two earlier. Robins apparently lack the incredibly accurate wristwatches of Capistrano's Swallows, as the exact date of Redbreast arrival varies, with the weather, from year to year. Yet across decades a remarkable stability can emerge. At Williamstown, Massachusetts, for example, the average date of spring's first Robin from 1816 to1838 was March 15; a century later, during the years 1916 to 1938, the average was again March 15!

Springtime Storms

One unfortunate by-product of early migration is the threat presented by sudden snowstorms which, trailing warm spells, may strike after the birds have already arrived at their breeding grounds. Should these storms consist of icy winds and heavy snows that batter the birds for several days in succession, the elements may prove fatally harsh. Indeed, numerous cases are on record where March blizzards in northern locales have killed Robins by the hundreds and thousands.

Even mild snowfalls can blanket local food supplies and thus create problems for early migrants who, now on their own territories, are loathe to return South. Under these conditions, Robins become opportunists and quickly exploit any windfall of foodstuff that happens their way. Thus Redbreasts will readily flock to birdfeeders supplied by friendly humans, and the tiniest patch of bare grass is hunted over and over again by every Robin in town. Once after an April snowstorm in New Hampshire, Robins even flocked around farmland manure heaps to prey upon the hordes of flying insects that had gathered there in dungful delight.

Naturally, Robins are not entirely altruistic when feeding at close quarters upon limited food supplies. Once after a kind-hearted birdwatcher overturned a clump of worm-writhing earth in an otherwise snowy field, a male Robin greedily claimed the mound as his own. When not chasing other birds away from his treasure chest, the piggish Redbreast ate so much that finally he could not even close his beak. When last seen, the selfish squatter was crouched atop the wiggling stockpile with a worm dangling from his bill, still refusing to surrender his claim.

Whether springtime snows are lethal or merely hardships, they raise the question of why Robins go north so early in the first place. Why don't Redbreasts simply remain in the South, with its warm temperatures and adequate food supplies, until the last remnants of winter have vanished from northern breeding grounds? Actually, the timing of spring migration represents a delicate balance between the advantages and disadvantages of an early trip. The sooner the birds get back north, the sooner they can establish territories, select mates, and breed; thus they can more easily raise two or even three broods during the upcoming season, with obvious benefits for the species. This advantage, however, must be weighed against the threat of late blizzards that can kill early migrants; indeed, even if the adults survive, the eggs and young of the season's first brood may be destroyed by springtime chills.

The Robins themselves, of course, do not ponder these matters when they test the air for signs of spring; their behavior is simply the product of natural selection. Those Robins with propensities for premature migration are weeded out of the population by the harsh wisdom of northern storms. Those Robins who have a tendency to migrate too late will, upon their arrival in the North, find all the attractive territories already occupied, and so will have difficulty in obtaining mates and breeding. Thus, although late migrators will not die like the premature migrators might, they will nonetheless be unable to pass on their tardy tendencies to other generations of Redbreasts.

Territorial Return

One of the most remarkable aspects of Robin migration is the return of individual birds to their previous breeding grounds. An eastern-bred bird, for example, would never migrate to the West in the spring, even though other Robins he wintered with may head off in a westerly direction. In one study, researchers found that about 55 percent of a group of Robins returned to the exact community where they had been hatched the year before; another 20 percent returned to within ten miles of their birthplace, and less than 10 percent settled one hundred or more miles away. Interestingly, all of the Robins who settled relatively far from their birthplaces chose more southern spots as their new homes (that is, they did not settle east, west, or north of their birthplaces). Perhaps during their return from the South these individuals were prematurely lured out of the migrating flock by some especially appealing terrain.

In any event, given the immensity of the Robin's potential breeding grounds (from coast to coast across Canada and the United States), these return figures are nothing less than incredible. How does a Robin find his way back to your backyard after spending the winter a thousand or more miles away? We can only speculate. Such gross navigational aids as the stars, sun, mountains, and rivers may guide him back to the state or province of his birthplace, and this is remarkable enough a feat in itself. But how can a year-old bird pick one backyard out of thousands when I get hopelessly lost going to a new supermarket on the other side of town? I wish I knew.

At least one thing seems clear, however. Robins—more particularly, the first-year birds—do not really return to their actual birthplaces so much as to the localities from which they disembarked for their first southern migration. Normally, these two places (birthplace vs. point of migratory departure) are virtually identical since the young birds do not wander any great distance from their nestsites before migrating in the fall. In one experiment, however, a Robin who had just left its nest was captured in Long Island, New York, and was then released seventy-five miles westward in Passaic, New Jersey. For the next three years, this bird returned to Passaic—not Long Island—after wintering in the South.

Not all Robins, by the way, are equally precise in reoccupying their old haunts, for there seem to be both sexual and age differences involved. In general, males are more likely than females to resettle the same territory as was held the previous season, and similarly, adults are more likely than first-year youngsters to return to the same spot as before. This is not to say that females, for example, are unknown to nest in the exact location—a certain tree, a particular porch—year after year after year; indeed, numerous such cases have been reported. But overall, both females and youngsters tend to return to the same general region of the previous season, but then settle wherever they find a suitable mate and/or territory.

Related to these differences in territorial return is the tendency toward both sexual and age separation during migration itself, for males in general precede the females, and adults in general precede first-year birds. For various reasons, these separations occur predominantly in the lower half of the continent (45°N latitude and below) and almost disappear by the time the Canadian provinces are reached. Interestingly, the birds' reproductive glands—whose enlargement seems to coincide with the start of spring migration—happen to expand in males before females, and in mature birds before those who hatched the year before.

In explaining the preceding of females by males, one turn-of-the-century ornithologist simply noted that the males migrate "in advance of their less hardy mates . . . to be followed by the females a week or so later when the weather is less severe" (Howe, 1898). Presumably that writer would have suggested a similar explanation for the migratory lagging shown by the "less hardy" Robin youngsters. In a less chauvinistic vein, however, the time-priority of males and grown-ups before females and adolescents ensures two beneficial effects: First, the early arriving males have time to secure their previous territories without having to simultaneously worry about wooing females (if territories and females were in flux concurrently, the poor males might wear themselves to a feathered frazzle). Secondly, the adults, who are of time-proven fitness, have first choice of northern nesting territories; in contrast, the less experienced first-year birds must contest among themselves for territories vacated by owners now deceased.

One final point about the Robin's faithful territorial return involves the functional isolation of breeding populations. Since Robins do not randomly resettle after migration but instead return to specific localities year after year, interbreeding across localities is relatively rare. Mountain systems in particular may reinforce this isolation effect; in one study, for example, researchers failed to find a single instance of a Robin who had hatched on one side of the Appalachian mountains breeding on the opposite side during successive seasons. Such lack of interbreeding among groups may have contributed to the evolution of the different races of Redbreast that now reside in various corners of the continent. Whether these races will continue to diverge until wholly distinct species are created is, of course, a matter of conjecture.

chapter 4

Of Property and Passion

The wooing of the Robin is a disappointment to believers in romance. There are no grotesque dances, such as highlight the courtship of many bird species; no fights over females, no song that is exclusively a mating call. In the practical mind of the male Robin, a choice of territory looms far more important than a choice of mate. Under such haphazard arrangements, a Robin may get together with the mate he had the previous summer. Then again, he may not.

—Trenary, 1954

Many Robin fanciers may violently object to Trenary's harsh synopsis of Robin courtship. For although the mating of Redbreasts is frequently conducted with restrained discretion (to the great frustration of voyeurish ornithologists), it can alternatively involve a variety of romantic exchanges between the participants. On one point, however, Trenary is indubitably correct: Robins (of *both* sexes) are landowners first and lovers only second. Mating, to be sure, is an indispensable delight without which Robins would lead an extremely ephemeral existence. But evidence strongly suggests that the male Robin becomes more attached to his territory than to his spouse, and that the female is similarly more loyal to her nesting premises than to her nesting partner.

Territory

Territoriality—the tendency to form strong attachments to a given area of space and to defend that area against intruders—is a trait which Robins display almost exclusively during their breeding season. By one account, Robins who were wintering on the Stanford University campus in California appeared to stake out territories as individualized feeding areas, but such behavior during the nonbreeding season is extremely exceptional. More typically, male Robins only select territories when they reach their northern breeding grounds in spring (often before the females have arrived in strength), defend it with the help of their mates throughout the summer, and then relinquish their claims when fall descends.

Although the average Robin territory is about a half acre in size, larger properties are possible where population pressures are weak (that is, where Robins are few in number), and smaller territories occur where such pressures are great. Usually those males who are first to appear North try to claim much larger areas than they will later be able to hold after the other local residents have arrived. Interestingly, even after all the residents have resettled a given region, several attractive areas will remain unclaimed regardless of population pressures. These areas are communal feeding grounds which are open to the public and cannot be privately owned. Dozens of local Redbreasts will regularly gather to forage at such locations, which typically lie on football fields, cemetery lawns, golf courses, or other wide stretches of short-cropped grass.

Although the boundaries of a given territory often follow distinct topographical features—a street, a building, a row of hedges—the borders sometimes run inexplicably down the centers of open lawns. In general, the owners have claim to every resource existing within those borders (nesting sites, building materials, bathing areas, and food), but such rights are by no means inviolable. Trespassing by neighboring Redbreasts, for example, occurs quite frequently. In addition, Robin territories sometimes overlap, especially in densely populated areas, so that a given piece of real estate might be shared by two different pairs of birds. Apparently the situation can occasionally get even more complicated, for once a pair of Robins in New Jersey held "nesting rights" in a certain tree even though another pair of Redbreasts possessed the "foraging rights" to the surrounding lawn.

Characteristics of Territoriality

Through the course of studying a wide variety of animals, scientists have constructed a classic model of territorial traits. According to this model, for example, an animal fighting within its own territory is nearly invincible against all intruding challengers. Thus,

> in all territorial species, without exception, possession of a territory lends enhanced energy to the proprietor. . . . The challenger is almost invariably defeated, the intruder expelled. In part, there seems some mysterious flow of energy and resolve which invests a proprietor on his home grounds. But likewise, so marked is the inhibition lying on the intruder, so evident his sense of trespass, we may be permitted to wonder if in all territorial species there does not exist . . . some universal recognition of territorial rights. (Ardrey, 1966)

Not surprisingly, one corollary of this invincibility principle is that an animal becomes progressively less successful the farther it fights from the center of its property.

Other characteristics of the classic territorial mode include: (1) males are, with few exceptions, more territorially inclined than females; (2) territorial aggression does not generally occur interspecifically—that is, between members of two different species ("A squirrel does not regard a mouse as a trespasser," in Ardrey's words); and (3) a territorial animal is seldom aggressive when meeting conspecifics outside of its territory.

Robins, who seem to have been largely overlooked by students of territorial behavior, do not match the above model very well. And nowhere is their disdain for such scientific generalities more blatant than regarding the widely accepted notion of territorial invincibility. As notorious trespassers, for example, Redbreasts seldom show much respect for the "territorial rights" of their neighbors. Secondly, Robins are not always—nor nearly always—successful in repelling intruders, for the latter may actually win 30 percent of all territorial clashes. Thirdly, property owners are sometimes remarkably tolerant of freshly discovered trespassers, and may not even confront the intruders at all.

In short, although Robins do benefit by fighting on their home ground (winning 70 percent of the contests occurring therein), they are by no means omnipotent. While many invaders are expelled, many others are either ignored or unsuccessfully fought. In the latter instances, landowners seem to retain their properties by simply remaining within them while the unrepelled invaders move leisurely onward (though frequently not victorious, proprietors are only rarely defeated to the point of surrendering their territories to challengers). Property attachment, therefore, is just as important as combat proficiency in the territorial aptitude of the Robin.

Robins, by the way, do conform nicely to at least one aspect of the invincibility principle—namely, that fighting success declines as a bird strays farther and farther from the center of its territory. Thus Robins win over 80 percent of the disputes occurring in the middle of their properties, compared to 60 percent at the territorial boundaries and only about 30 percent a hundred yards beyond those boundaries. Apparently, whatever underlies the home-ground advantage does not vanish abruptly at the property's borders but instead dissipates only gradually as a function of distance from the territorial center.

As mentioned earlier, territorial behavior in most species characterizes the male rather than the female (a few exceptions include Horned Owls and Ring-tailed Lemurs, in whom territories are defended by both sexes; Button Quail, in whom females alone are territorial; and wolves and humans, who often defend territorial borders as groups of individuals). In Robins, the female is definitely territorially minded. The male, admittedly, establishes the territory initially and thereafter makes many more territorial defenses than does the female, who is after all pressed by the duties of nest-building and egg-incubation. But the female is perfectly capable of maintaining a territory entirely by herself and will indeed do so should her mate suddenly disappear during a given nesting cycle.

Interestingly, the two sexes show some differences regarding the advantage accrued by fighting on home ground. Females win about 75 percent of the fights occurring within their own territories compared to only 20 percent in the territories of opponents, while males win less than 70 percent of the fights in their own territories compared to about 45 percent within the properties of opponents. Clearly, the home-ground advantage is a much more potent force for female Robins than for males.

Another sexual difference in the aggression of Robins is that males seem to be a bit dominant over females. There are exceptions, of course, as in the case of a one-eyed fellow who—perhaps because of his handicap—was consistently henpecked by his unsympathetic spouse. But as far as territorial defense is concerned, males win approximately 65 percent of all disputes occurring between the sexes.

Robins, then, present a much more complex picture of sex

differences in territoriality than seems to be portrayed in most other species. The males initially establish the territories and then have primary responsibility in its defense; nevertheless, the somewhat subordinate females do contribute significantly to the effort. And while both sexes benefit from fighting within their own territories, it is the females, rather than the males, who show the home-ground advantage most strongly.

The third general characteristic of territorial behavior—the lack of strife between animals who belong to different species— does not apply to the Robin any better than the concepts of invincibility and male exclusiveness. Although Redbreasts tolerate the presence of many non-Robin animals in their territories, they will with regularity drive certain species from their nesting areas. Not surprisingly, many of these repelled animals are among the Robin's traditional enemies. Thus Robins will attack Jays, Crows, and squirrels, all of whom loot Robin nests of eggs and young; cats and dogs, who are major threats to flightless Robin youngsters just out of their nests; hawks and owls, who prey upon young and old Robins alike; Grackles, who not only compete with Robins for nesting sites but also try to puncture their eggs; and the female Cowbird, a social parasite who often tries to sneak her own egg into an unattended Robin's nest. Other birds who are normally ignored may be bullied by a greedy Redbreast under special competitive circumstances, such as at a crowded birdfeeder, but this is not usually considered territorial behavior. Of course, Robins themselves are sometimes attacked by other species, such as the territorial Mockingbird and Wood Thrush, and frequently the scrappy English Sparrow, with whom the much larger Redbreast usually seems unable to cope.

The final territorial characteristic mentioned earlier—a prevailing lack of aggression between individuals who meet outside of their territories—is most certainly untrue of Robins. Indeed, Redbreasts may be quite quarrelsome even when great distances from their nestsites. For example, at the communal feeding grounds where dozens of individuals may gather for breakfast, scuffles are not at all scarce even though, somewhat paradoxically, the birds generally try to avoid direct confrontations.

Aggressive Behaviors

Robins brandish many bellicose behaviors. Each of these, of course, may occasionally appear in some context other than territorial dispute, such as mate rivalry, birdfeeder squabbling, or periodic flares of temper wherever Robins happen to flock together. Nevertheless, aggressiveness in Redbreasts is most frequently ignited by the fires of territoriality.

One common hostile gesture that Robins employ is the *tail lift,* in which the aggressor humbles head and raises rump to issue a threat of battle. A similar warning is conveyed by the *crouch,* in which the individual's whole body is simply lowered to the ground or a perch. To complement either of these postures, or to communicate displeasure from even a normal stance, Robins may repeatedly open and shut their empty mandibles and thereby produce a *bill-snap* sound that is likely to intimidate any nearby foe. Alternatively, the birds may simply hold their beaks open in a wide gaping gesture. Both the *gape* and the bill-snap, of course, probably represent "intention movements" which indicate the performer's willingness to bite an opponent.

Singing is yet another behavioral weapon in the Robin's arsenal. Although "song duels" of the sort found in some birds have not been reported for Robins specifically, the male Redbreast's carol is nonetheless believed to deter other males from entering the singer's territory. This behavior can thus fulfill its antagonistic function even in the complete absence of visual contact between two birds. The male's carol, by the way, probably also serves to attract eligible females to the crooner's corner.

A somewhat more dynamic form of aggression is the *push* (also called *supplanting),* which is most frequently demonstrated when one Robin approaches another on the ground through a series of intermittent bursts of running. As the aggressing individual repeatedly nears the other bird, the latter repeatedly scampers off a few yards in hasty retreat. Should pushing be performed among the treetops, the aggressor simply flies toward his thereupon-fleeing opponent and then lands on or near the perch which the latter has just vacated. In either case, the pursuer—armed with a strange repelling force like that arising between the "like" poles of two magnets—employs proximity to shove the other bird away. When occurring within the pusher's territory, the chase sequence ends as soon as a property boundary is crossed, for then the landowner stops the pursuit.

Nip-'n-tuck flying is a sort of pushing that's gotten out of hand. Here, one bird flies hard on the heels of another at seemingly top speed, the pair at first skimming just above the ground, then weaving between trees and bushes, now curling into upward rolls like virtuoso flyers of World War I vintage. Screaming all the while, the two may soon be joined by several others to form a contagious dogfight of angry Red Barons.

All of the aggressive behaviors described so far involve little if any physical contact; their effects, though usually sufficient to induce fleeing by the aggressed-against individual, are strictly psychological. Nitty gritty combat can occur, however, as in the case of *wing-jousting.* In this engagement, two contestants initially face each other on the ground, a yard or so apart; then, as if signaled by some invisible referee, they simultaneously fly up together, buffeting with wings, clawing with feet, and biting with beaks. Rising ten to twenty feet in their furious breast-to-breast battle, the birds soon tumble back to the ground, reorient toward each other, and joust again and again until one knight yields by simply wandering away. For all its fury, jousting seldom results

in any real damage beyond plucked feathers and bruised wings.

A final aggressive display, this one far more notable for its flare than effectiveness, is *shadow-boxing.* Whenever a Robin flies, hops, or perches near a well-washed window or super-shiny hubcap, he is inevitably confronted with the redbreasted "intruder" reflected therein. Responding to the challenge, the bird begins to buffet and peck his image quite mercilessly, whereupon his spunky opponent usually replies in kind. Sometimes sparring thus for days, the indefatigable featherweight only occasionally retires to some neutral corner for food between rounds. One persistent pugilist in Kansas City skirmished with his glassy silhouette for sixteen days in March, and only interrupted the struggle for brief food forays and periodic withdrawals "to his telephone wire for rest and contemplation." Another stubborn Spartan, this one on Detroit's Belle Isle Park, dueled and dashed against a gas station's windowpane for the better part of one April. Throughout his thirty days' war, he

> was kept pretty busy, without being able to administer a knockout blow. After each attack the hated enemy would spring up as peppery as before. The female during this time remained on the lower limb of a nearby tree, occasionally making remarks. (Wilson, 1919)

I can well imagine what she was saying. And with good cause, for shadow-boxing is quite as costly as it is foolish. Not only is the male prevented from tending to more serious family business, but he is typically distracted to dangerous degrees; indeed, a cat can sometimes approach within mere feet of the heedless and, perhaps soon, headless fighter. At the very least, the bulldoggish battering not only bloodies the boxer but blunts his beak as well. How can a truce be enforced upon an image-punching Robin? Well, a murky screen over the window should ward off the bellicose reflection, while a shiny hubcap can be wheeled into a garage or else out of the Redbreast's beloved territory.

We might now digress somewhat and consider an interesting notion concerning the Robin's red breast. Many animals, it seems, automatically respond with hostility to the mere sight of a certain part of a conspecific's body. A male Stickleback fish, for example, becomes belligerent as soon as it sees the red throat of another male. The crucial importance of the red throat is revealed by the fact that the male will not attack a female Stickleback (females do not have the redness) but will attack an object that does not resemble a fish at all but which happens to be colored red on its underside. A male Stickleback, for instance, once became quite aggressive toward a red-bottomed truck as it drove past a window near the fish's aquarium.

As another example of this principle, the English Robin is triggered into aggressiveness by the sight of another Robin's red breast. Thus conspecifics whose breasts are experimentally painted brown will be completely ignored by the little bird; in contrast, a mere tuft of red feathers mounted on a perch will be attacked rather vehemently. Still other examples of such aggression-eliciting cues include the black "moustache" which is sported by the male American Flicker, the deep blue throat that decorates the neck of the European Emerald Lizard, and the purple-and-white arms of the male Cuttlefish.

No one yet has conclusively demonstrated that our American Robin responds aggressively to simply the sight of another Robin's red breast; still, it seems probable that the species does not differ significantly from the English Robin in this respect. This would explain why a Robin becomes trapped into sparring with a window (since the glass persistently reflects the bird's own red breast back to him); why wing-jousting—which seems to represent nearly equal aggressiveness in two combatants— only occurs after both birds have directly faced each other (since this is the only orientation which permits both birds to simultaneously view each other's breast); and why juvenile Robins appear to be seldom attacked by adults (since the breasts of youngsters are largely spotted and possess little if any red coloring). In sum, it may well be that the very heart of aggression among Robins lies in the Redbreasts' red breasts.

Benefits of Territoriality

Most of the benefits that Robins gain by being territorial derive from the dispersal effects that territoriality imposes upon their population. True, Robin territories can both compress and overlap, and thus do not scatter the birds as effectively as they otherwise might. Nevertheless, Redbreasts are still more spaced out as a result of their territoriality than they would be without it.

One obvious potential advantage of population spacing is retardation of the spread of contagious diseases. As we shall see in Chapter 10, however, Robins largely negate this benefit by sleeping in dense flocks each summer evening. But if territorial spacing does not make Robins more resistant to disease, it at least makes their nests less susceptible to predation. Finding one Robin's nest, for example, does not in the least aid a Crow or squirrel in the discovery of another Robin's nest; in fact, finding one nest practically ensures that another will not be found nearby. Thus predators cannot go on rampages of mass destruction and rob dozens of nests in a single afternoon or evening, as might instead be the case were Robins to breed in tight colonies.

Another benefit of population spacing is to help ensure that Robins do not deplete the food supplies existing within a given area. Although food scarcity is seldom an overwhelming problem for nonbreeding Robins who are generally mobile enough to find greener pastures, food resources become of paramount importance during the nesting season when parents as well as young are anchored to specific localities. By spacing their nests, however,

Robins can find considerable food for both themselves and their ever-hungry young within their respective territories. Robins, remember, abandon their territoriality during most of the non-breeding season; thus territoriality and breeding seem to go hand in hand.

A more subtle benefit linking territoriality to food availability and breeding involves the incubation duties of the female Robin. Throughout the two-week incubation period, the female obviously needs to obtain nourishment and yet cannot leave her eggs unwatched and unwarmed during extended food-gathering excursions. In many avian species, the male solves this problem by feeding his mate as she sits on the nest. The male Robin, being perhaps too busy patrolling his territory, seldom if ever serves dinner to his mate; nonetheless, the fact that he does maintain a territory helps abate the female's dilemma. By discouraging the presence of other Robins in the immediate nesting vicinity, the male fences off an area in which his mate need not compete with other Redbreasts when she interrupts her sitting to feed. Consequently she doesn't have to stray far in search of food, and thus she is able to keep her time off the nest minimally brief.

Another possible benefit deriving from territorial spacing is the functional isolation of mating pairs, whereby each couple is permitted to conduct family business without undue interference from other Robins. Without territorial restrictions, unmated individuals might be forever attempting to seduce one member of an already established pair. Such temptations, obviously, would hardly be conducive to the stable sort of family situation needed to rear young.

Competition among nestlings is perhaps even more dangerous to family stability than is mate-rivalry. In one unusual case where two females nested side by side after mating with a bigamous male, one set of eggs hatched a full week before the other set. Unfortunately, the bigger and more vigorous older nestlings—who could clamor for food much more insistently than their newly hatched neighbors—dominated the attention of both mothers so completely that the neglected batch of infants soon died. Here, then, was a type of family interference that territorial spacing most assuredly helps to minimize.

There are two other possible benefits that territoriality bestows upon Robins, but neither involves population spacing effects. One utility derives from the fact that Robins, by constantly patrolling their properties, become intimate with the characteristics of the terrain therein. This familiarity may offer several advantages to the landowner, not the least of which is some sort of "confidence" inherently arising from fighting in familiar rather than strange surroundings; in other words, familiarity-caused confidence may underlie the home-ground advantage effects that were described earlier. Detailed acquaintance with the nesting area may also offer the Robin some measure of security against predators, since the bird knows at any given instant where best to hide when danger threatens.

Territory can also serve to select the "best" Robins for breeding. This is so because the female Robin seems to be more attracted to the property a male holds than to the male himself. Should, for example, her original mate suffer a *coup d'état* and be dispossessed of his holdings (which rarely, but sometimes, happens), the female usually accepts the new lord quite readily rather than following the vanquished male into exile. Certainly male Robins who are not strong and bold enough to hold territories are unlikely to obtain mates. It may further be that the most desirable territories—presumably held by the best males— are competitively sought by the females as well; thus territory could mediate a system whereby the best males breed with the best females.

Mating

Although spring normally marks the initiation of sexual activity in Robins, some individuals occasionally cast good sense to the wind and attempt mating during winter months. Once, Robins who were migrating through Berkeley, California, repeatedly engaged in sporadic copulatory behavior even though February had only just begun. Even more extraordinary are instances of premature breeding that have included midwinter nesting attempts. One pair of Redbreasts in Ellwood City, Pennsylvania, managed to fill a nest with three eggs during an unusually mild December. With the onset of January, however, came five-inch snowfalls that virtually inundated the nest. Nevertheless, the shivering female—who was able to eat at a nearby birdfeeder which her mate guarded against other birds—remained on her eggs a full seventeen days. Unfortunately, the noble efforts of these would-be parents were in vain, for the eggs—probably killed by the cold—never hatched.

Somewhat better success was achieved by another pair of January nesters who managed to hatch three eggs in downtown Columbus, Ohio. For two days thereafter, relatively warm weather permitted the parents to find enough worms (the only food available) to feed their youngsters, but a sudden drop to 12°F drove the annelids far beneath the frozen ground and doomed the hapless infants. These Robins, by the way, had nested across the street from a large display involving thousands of Christmas lights. In view of the fact that "unnatural" lighting conditions have been known to induce breeding in numerous animals (for example, pheasants, rats, and trout), it was possible that the Christmas lights had prompted the Columbian Redbreasts to breed prematurely.

Even when Robins wait for the proper season to breed, their mating behavior may in fact be quite improper. Robins, for example, are overwhelmingly monogamous creatures who normally are devoted to only one mate at a time; every once in a while, however, polygamy manages to rear its lusty rump. Such marital exceptions always seem to take the form of polygyny (that is, two females and only one male), as no cases of two males mated to one female have ever been reported. Nor, for that matter, have there been reports of any frolicking foursomes.

When two females mate with one male, they may either build separate nests, sometimes one right next to the other, or they may actually build a single nest to hold both sets of eggs. In the latter case, the females must agree upon some satisfactory plan for incubating their eggs, and for this they usually follow one of two different procedures. Some pairs of females incubate in equal shifts, with one bird periodically relieving the other; others, however, prefer to sit simultaneously side by side or, if the nest is too cramped for that, to piggyback one another in mountainous maternal majesty.

The fact that Robins are primarily monogamous, of course, need not imply that they mate for life. Many different birds do so—including lovebirds, pigeons, geese, swans, and most birds of prey—but Robins, alas, do not. True, Robins, who usually rear two or three broods per summer, almost always remain tied to the same spouse for successive broods within a single season. But from one year to the next, males and females tend to get as scrambled as Sunday morning eggs. In fact, only the faithful return of both sexes to their previous territories permits any chance of successive remating at all; that is, since both males and females return to the same northern locality each spring (as opposed to resettling at random places throughout the continent), chance rematings are at least possible. Nevertheless, these "accidents" are thought to characterize only one out of every eight or so pairs of returning Redbreasts.

In any event, the longest record of remating in Robins appears to be held by a pair who nested for three successive years in Columbus, Ohio. This relatively devoted couple was particularly interesting because during the spring of the third year the male was initially seen in the company of a strange, early-arriving female instead of his previous mate. Within a few days, however, his old flame had returned and the newcomer, perhaps not coincidentally, had disappeared. Thus,

> it may well be that a female Robin, on returning and finding her place pre-empted, does not calmly accept the situation and go elsewhere, as does the Song Sparrow female, but that she drives off her rival. (Nice, 1933)

Relatively little is known about the courtship behavior of the Robin. Much of the problem is that the birds' wooing appears under so many different guises that generalizations concerning its nature are extremely evasive. The following first-hand accounts, beginning with some observations of John Audubon, readily convey the wide variety of courtship strategies which a male Robin may employ:

> I have often seen him at the earliest dawn of a May morning, strutting around her with all the pomposity of a pigeon. Sometimes along a space of ten to twelve yards, he is seen with his tail fully spread, his wings shaking and his throat inflated, running over the grass and brushing it, until he nears his mate; (next) he moves round her several times without once rising from the ground. She then receives his caresses. (Audubon, 1856)

The male's pomposity, however, may evolve into gladiatorial maneuvers should a rival suddenly intrude. Thus one snowy April morn did a woman in Danvers, Massachusetts, watch a male Robin approach a female just as another male landed near her. Outraged, the first bird attacked and

> with a loud cry drove the interloper around the corner of the house. But as he turned the corner in hot pursuit a gust of the April breeze caught him sidewise, whirled him about, and drove him back over a strip of ice that

gave him no footing, though his feet moved rapidly in the effort to overtake his rival.... Then he looked to his female only to find that his rival, who had flown over the house and back to the trysting place, was with her again. With a shrill scream of rage the baffled suitor flew at his rival with open mouth, driving him from the vicinity. (Quoted by Forbush, 1929)

Things may get even more hectic when a single female attracts a bevy of males. Describing what he called "Robin racket," naturalist John Burroughs wrote of

trains of three or four birds rushing pell-mell over the lawn and fetching up in a tree or bush, or occasionally upon the ground, all piping and screaming at the top of their voices, but whether in mirth or anger it is hard to tell. The nucleus of the train is a female. One cannot see that the males in pursuit of her are rivals; it seems rather as if they had united to hustle her out of the place. But somehow the matches are no doubt made and sealed during these mad rushes. (Quoted by Tyler, 1949)

Apparently, such behavior—which is obviously similar to the nip-'n-tuck flying described earlier—can be either territorial or romantic in nature.

Finally, Robin courtship may be neither pompous, chivalrous, nor raucous, but instead simply serene. The following description of a Robin suitor comes from ornithologist Bradford Torrey:

How gently he approaches his beloved! How carefully he avoids ever coming disrespectfully near! No sparrow-like screaming, no dancing about, no melodramatic gesticulation. If she moves from one side of the tree to the other, or to the tree adjoining, he follows in silence. Yet every movement is a petition, an assurance that his heart is hers and ever must be. (Quoted by Tyler, 1949)

All of the above observations, of course, deal with the preliminaries of mating rather than with its consummation. The latter is usually a restrained, uninspiring joining that evinces little in the way of fiery desire by either participant. More specifically, the female simply crouches on either the ground or a perch and is briefly mounted by the male, who—fanning his wings for balance—presses his cloaca against that of his mate.

Occasionally, however, a bird succumbs to the pleasures of passion and veritably sizzles in a frantic fit of frenzied fervor. One male in Baltimore, for example, repeatedly mounted one of his own offspring (of unknown gender) during its first day out of the nest. While the wide-eyed youngster froze in squatted stupefaction, its overly affectionate father copulated no less than four times during one satisfying if exhausting thirty-second period. In a comparable account, a female once tried to mount one of her own fledglings; this was particularly interesting since the normal sexual behavior of female Robins involves squatting, not mounting.

Then there was the case of an ardent male who went berserk in the face of unrequited passion. This fellow

> advanced on the female with his wings slightly open, bill gaping, and body feathers extended, and tried to mount. She drove him away with a vicious peck. The male then mounted an earth clump, fanned his wings vigorously as he tried to copulate with it, then ran and tried to mount the female again. She dodged and ran a few steps; the male then tried to copulate with a piece of crumpled newspaper, again fanning his wings vigorously, then went to the female and attempted to mount from the front, but was again driven off. He returned once more; this time the female squatted and he mounted, apparently successfully. The female then violently attacked him and chased him away, the two flying out of sight in a long, twisting flight. (Young, 1949)

Other examples of Robin debauchery include an immature bird who, apparently smoking with passion, tried to mate with a package of cigarettes; two females who attacked a male after the latter unwisely ignored their squatting invitations to copulate; and a male who, during pitched battle with another male, suddenly grabbed his opponent by the neck and then mounted him with dishonorable intentions. (The surprise maneuver worked, for the assaulted bird promptly fled in mortified retreat.)

In closing this account of the Robin's mating habits, we should perhaps simply emphasize that the bulk of our discussion has focused on exceptional rather than typical behavior. For most Robins, mating is strictly a spring and summertime sport that is played with only two on a team, and seldom with the same partner from one year to the next. Courtship—while sometimes showy—more often goes unwitnessed by humans, and copulation—while occasionally misdirected—is more often brusque, businesslike, and to the point. Robins are, after all, lovers only second.

chapter 5

Cradles of Love

Hanging from one side of the Robin's nest are two fringed white satin badges, fastened by mud and sticks. They bear the seal of New York and the words, "New York N.E.A. at Boston, 1903." We have found that these badges were worn at a national educational convention held in Boston. A little to the left of these badges, near the rim of the nest, is a knot of coarse white lace, not merely woven over and under the grass, but artistically coiled about the outside and securely fastened with mud and tiny sticks. Through this lace, woven in and out through its coarse mesh as neatly as any human being could do it, are two white chicken feathers. The rest of this remarkable nest is decorated with long pieces of string; white string, brown and yellow string, a piece of blue embroidery silk, the hem of a fine handkerchief and a bit of white satin ribbon. Turned upside down, the nest gives one the impression of a bonnet with satin strings and trimmed with a little knot of white lace and two white quills. A truly wonderful nest!

—Katharine S. Parsons, 1906

Robins build nests from Mexico to northern Canada, from the Atlantic to the Pacific coast, from sea level to 12,000 feet in altitude. Obviously this impressive distribution suggests that the Robin can successfully adapt to a wide range of different nesting environments. Since flexible acceptance of breeding conditions is an important aspect of an animal's ability to withstand destructive pressures exerted against its population, Robins must in this regard be considered one of evolution's best accomplishments.

Nesting, of course, involves selection of an appropriate site as well as actual construction of the nest itself, and for the Robin, these two tasks entail separate sets of environmental requirements. What these requirements are and how they are negotiated make up one of the most interesting chapters in the Robin's life cycle.

Site Selection

Selection of the nesting site, a matter of considerable deliberation for most Robins, is a chore primarily undertaken by the female. True, the male may occasionally offer a suggestion or two by bringing nest-building materials to a certain spot. But such recommendations will likely as not be declined by the finicky female. In one case like this, a Massachusetts male began repairing a previously used nest only to have his wishes adamantly ignored by his mate, who eventually chose a site some distance away. In picking the site, the female may appraise several possibilities by lowering herself onto each one as if testing for sufficient room. She may then betray a bit of indecision by beginning nest construction at two separate places before settling on her final choice.

This choice is generally some five to twenty feet above the ground, although sites on the ground itself or as high as sixty feet are sometimes used. Concealment does not appear to be a crucial requirement—indeed, Robin nests are often among the easiest in birddom to locate—but a firm foundation is of paramount importance. The Robin's *statant nest* is supported primarily from below (in contrast to *suspended nests* which are supported from the rims or sides), and so is usually built upon a sturdy branch, fork, or crotch of a tree. In this respect, old orchard and shade trees suit the Robin's needs particularly well.

Concealment does play some role in site selection, of course. Robins, who rear two or three broods of young each season, usually employ separate nests for each brood. And largely due to considerations of concealment, the first nest—built in early spring when many deciduous trees are still leafless—is most frequently constructed among the branches of evergreens. For the season's second brood, however, most females prefer the now-foliated (and thicker-limbed), deciduous trees for housing their nests.

Nesting Neighbors

Since Robins defend their nesting territory against other Robins, side-by-side nesting by two pairs of Redbreasts almost never occurs. There are, however, many instances of Robins congenially nesting with other species in the same tree, with two nests sometimes as little as a foot apart. Thus Robins have been known to nest simultaneously with Kingbirds, Orchard Orioles, and Warbling Vireos, all in the same tree and all successful in rearing their young. As long as these different species do not heavily compete for identical food resources, such associations may not be significantly disadvantageous. Peculiar problems, though, can arise. Once in a Pennsylvanian evergreen grove, a Purple Grackle's nest was found to contain not only two Grackle eggs but a Robin egg as well. Apparently, the Robin who had built her nest in the same grove accidentally visited the wrong nest at the wrong time.

Another case of mix-up between avian neighbors involved some Robins who had nested only nine feet from the homestead of a pair of Kingbirds. The two species got along fine until a bird-banding ornithologist decided to approach the Kings' nestlings.

Perceiving potential peril, the male Robin perched near the menaced nest and began issuing vigorous warnings to the oncoming human. But instead of supporting the defense, the thankless Daddy Kingbird promptly pecked his neighbor's noggin until the startled samaritan abandoned the altruistic affray. Presumably the Robin had gotten too close to the King's babies!

Some nesting neighbors can be more than mere nuisances, however. English Sparrows, diminutive in size but colossal in spirit, sometimes badger nesting Robins until they move elsewhere to make their home. And Blue Jays, those egg-stealing archenemies of Robins, almost never make welcome or even tolerated neighbors. Indeed, the two species usually fight whenever they meet. In one informative exception to this general rule, however, a pair of Robins once nested in the same tree as a pair of Jays. With at least one sentry always on guard at the nest, the cautious Redbreasts eventually succeeded in fledging their young. But their cause was even more notably aided by a local outbreak of inchworms on which both bird families could readily feast. Very likely, such superabundancy of suppers not only reduced the Robins' tendency to drive the Blue Jays away, but at the same time decreased the Jays' motivation to rob Robin nests.

Comparable increases in tolerance among normally antagonistic species frequently develop amid prey-a-plenty. Both hawks and owls, for example, uncharacteristically endure the presence of other raptors (both of their own species and of others as well) wherever runaway rodent populations arise. This process of antipathy reduction, which permits a greater density of predators to coexist within a given area, is one of Nature's mechanisms for controlling local outbreaks by such prey species as rodents and inchworms.

Artificial Sites

While some Robins nest deep in the forest, the majority build on the outskirts of woods and, as almost everyone has observed, in bushes and trees within human-inhabited areas. Often these sites are not merely near our constructions but actually upon them, sometimes causing considerable (though readily accepted) inconvenience to the landlords. Thus city construction has been halted while Robin tenants nested on girders, telephone booths have been closed while Robins raised young atop the dial box, house painters have been routed by irate and fretful bird parents, school children have been relegated to backdoor entrances while Mother Robin sat watch in front, and burly policemen have been reduced to whispering, goggle-eyed godfathers during the five-week period that nesting Robins invaded headquarters. Robins have even gone so far as to nest, quite successfully, within the pocket of a coat left hanging on a garden tree by a forgetful musician.

Robins, furthermore, do not even insist that their nesting sites remain absolutely stationary. One mother-to-be in Ithaca, New York, reared four babies atop a steel crane which constantly swung back and forth to load cinders aboard railroad cars. "It must be like life on ocean waves," a metaphorical crane operator remarked at the time. Another and even more incredible example of the Robin's acceptance of mobile homes—perhaps a bit too incredible, come to think of it—was reported by the *New York Times* in 1946. According to the *Times,* a Robin both constructed and egged a nest on a Chicago & Northwestern locomotive in Sioux City, Iowa. Even though the engine chugged here and there every once in a while, the unperturbed Redbreast managed to accomplish her motherly chores by following the train throughout its meandering jaunts.

The Robin's ready acceptance of all these unnatural nesting sites, by the way, strengthens a point made earlier—namely, that Robins show considerable adaptiveness in their tolerance of nesting conditions. An occasional individual, to be sure, may reveal marked inability to adjust to a particular environment,

especially if that environment defies "natural" laws. Take for example the case of the Robin who built her nest on the south end of a shed covering a turntable upon which the direction of a train locomotive could be reversed. When the south end of the shed was turned north, the unthinking bird simply built another nest on the "new" south end. Since the shed rotated periodically from day to day, the obliging Robin soon had two nests and two sets of eggs, and at last accounts was incubating whichever nest happened to be facing south at the time. This poor female obviously lacked enough insight regarding the nature of her situation to successfully adapt. Yet were she not as adaptable as she in fact was, she would not have tried nesting in such a strange setting as a railroad yard in the first place!

This perky propensity of the Robin for choosing people-infested sites seems to be encouraged by at least three factors. First and foremost, during the breeding season Robins are not nearly as timid as many other bird species, and are not easily frightened by humans. Nesting Robins, in fact, make excellent subjects for nature photographers who are frequently permitted to take close-ups that other species simply find intolerable.

A second factor is the greater amount of Robin-type food that probably exists in cultivated areas. Worm-filled lawns, of course, are especially attractive to Robins. And more particularly, food is always a dominating concern of nesting Robins since their babies consume enormous amounts as they grow toward independence.

Thirdly, many of our buildings, bridges, and fences provide nesting sites that offer ample support and hence appear ideal to the critical eye of a scouting female. Sometimes there is a cornucopia of excellent sites, whereupon Mrs. Robin may embark upon a veritable orgy of nest-building. Years ago in Ohio, construction workers watched a Robin begin twenty-six separate nests in the spaces between a wooden girder and the roof rafters lying across it. After a week of self-indulgence among these irresistible sites—with workmen supplying building materials and placing bets on where the final functional nest would be—the female settled on one nest, laid eggs, and hatched them.

Unfortunately, such compulsive capers do not always conclude so well. Once a Robin started nests on five separate fire-escape steps, completed two of them, laid two eggs in one nest and one egg in the other, spent five days incubating both sets, and finally abandoned the whole endeavor. Such behavior, incidentally, serves well to remind us that Robins—like women and men—sometimes display considerable individual variation in their actions. Thus two Robins, faced with what appear to be essentially comparable situations (such as an abundance of attractive nesting sites), may respond in two completely different ways (one bird successfully settling on one site, the other abandoning all the sites in utter irresolution). Such individual differences may of course be extremely interesting. Yet they are not so satisfying to discover as are general principles or "laws" of Robin behavior, since recognition of these laws adds to our appreciation of the underlying orderliness that generally characterizes Nature.

Nest Construction

In nest construction, as with site selection, the female assumes primary responsibility. The male frequently brings materials to the site and may even help build to some extent, but more likely he will only drop his load haphazardly on the side of the emerging structure. On the whole, his mate makes more material-gathering trips (perhaps more than a hundred in a twelve-hour period), brings bigger loads (sometimes so clumsily large that all but her flapping wings disappear from front view), and does by far most of the actual construction (all of it, in many cases). In those instances where the male does pitch in, however,

he and his mate cooperate fairly closely, with one bird remaining at work on the nest until the partner returns with more building materials.

Robins usually take five or six days to build the nest for their first brood of the season, and then somewhat less (perhaps two or three days) for their second brood's nest later in the summer. The exact amount of time that nest-building takes, though, varies considerably among individual Robins, and the same bird—should her nest be destroyed as she is beginning to lay eggs—may build an entirely new nest within a single day. Like construction time, the size of the final product varies but generally measures six or seven inches across the top and three inches in height (the inside is about four inches wide and two-and-a-half inches deep).

Stages of Construction

The typical nest is built in three distinct stages. First, coarse grass, straw, leaves, rootlets, and occasionally pieces of paper or rags are formed into a firm foundation; slightly finer materials may be used to shape the sides. The Robin greatly prefers that these materials be wet when she builds, perhaps because they are then more pliable. After the nest's skeleton is erected, the female stands in its center and then circles, squats, and presses down with her wings until the nest is molded to the contour of her body.

The second stage of construction consists of an inner lining of mud that varies in thickness from an inch at the bottom to a quarter inch at the rim. In making this, the female brings pellets of mud in her bill, peppers them into the nest walls, and—having done this many times—gets into the nest, rotates her body, thumps her feet, and slaps her wings to beat the wet plaster into shape. Interestingly enough, Robins have been known to use the castings of earthworms (subterranean dirt that has been eaten and then excreted on the surface) as mud for their nests, even when "regular" mud was abundantly available.

The third and final stage of nest construction usually begins before the mud layer is entirely hardened. As her final touch, the female carpets her creation with fine, soft grasses which, as the mud dries, are soon cemented into smoothed fixity. Her cradle, now complete, is ready for occupancy.

Although these three stages typify the nest-building of Robins, exceptions to this general pattern are not entirely rare. Occasionally, the mud layer is completely omitted; or, the female may skip the soft lining almost as if she had run out of time before her eggs began to arrive. Robins also achieve a bit of variety over the ordinary construction procedures through an extravagant choice of materials, as markedly exemplified in the opening quote. Other revolutionary architects have used equally unlikely materials ranging from Christmas tree icicles to horse-hair. One female Redbreast, who was offered an abundant supply of cotton-cloth strips, ferried so darn much of the stuff to her nest that, in the words of an on-site observer, "the whole affair soon became an unmanageable mess and was eventually abandoned."

The three basic nest-building stages may also be modified if the female merely repairs an old nest rather than build a new one from scratch. While Robins don't usually use ready-made nests, they do occasionally reoccupy the same nest for successive broods within a season. In rarer cases, they use the same nest year after year. One extraordinary female, for instance, enjoyed the same nest for six consecutive years, with two broods per year, adding a new layer of material to the skyscraper structure each time.

Several bits of evidence suggest that such repetitive use of previous nests may not necessarily reflect fondness for a particular nest but rather loyalty to the site where the structure lies. More than one Robin, for example, has been known to lay her eggs on a bare window ledge in the same spot where earlier stood her nest, which had been removed by someone for some reason or other. In a similar vein, Robins frequently make repeated attempts to rebuild nests on a given site should the first nest be destroyed; in one instance, a female in Cambridge, Massachusetts, stubbornly constructed a total of five successive nests on a low-lying tree branch after a busybody human had removed each of the first four structures in hopes that Mrs. Robin would pick a new location less vulnerable to cats. Finally, nests on buildings seem to be reused more frequently than are nests in trees, probably because the former enjoy better support as well as more safety from squirrels, Jays, Crows, and other nest-attackers.

In addition to reusing their own nests, Robins occasionally reclaim old nests of other species (for example, Catbirds), albeit only after modifying the structure to their personal satisfaction. Much more frequently, other birds rear families in secondhand Robin nests. Mourning Doves in particular like to renovate Robin nests of seasons past; in some areas, as many as 20 percent of the Robin nests that remain intact over winter are used by Doves the following spring. (Indicative of the sturdiness of Robin tectonics, by the way, is the fact that almost half of all Robin nests are reusable from one year to the next—perhaps the highest such percentage for any songbird.) Occasionally Doves even try to pirate a nest that's in current use, in which case the owners may either meekly submit and move somewhere else, or staunchly defend what is rightfully theirs.

The Import of Moisture

Because Robins prefer mud and other wet materials for their nests, their building efforts are influenced to a large extent by the presence and absence of moisture in their immediate environment. Under normal conditions, the female tends to restrict her construction to early hours when morning dew blankets the ground. Should a summer dry spell occur, she and her neighbors will hold back on building activities, only to be thrown into a flurry of construction when the rains finally come. Sometimes, if the drought is severe, she may begrudgingly concede to the forces of Nature and build without mud.

Alternatively, she may respond with undaunted determination to build her nest in accordance with accepted Robin tradition. One ingenious female was observed to wet her feathers by birdbath immersions and then shake herself off on a nearby dusty road, thereby creating for herself what Mother Nature wouldn't. Another female adopted a similar solution but chose to reverse the process—she scooped dirt into her mouth and then dipped her bill in water before continuing nestward. These examples may say something about the Robin's resourcefulness, but they also comment on the importance of moisture during nest-erection.

Rain drops, though, are much like family relatives—they're quite all right if they visit in small numbers but if they arrive en masse they tend to overstay their welcome rather quickly. If rain persists after the Robin has completed her mud layer, she may delay lining her nest until the sun shines and permits the clay to harden. In localities where steady stretches of spring showers are not uncommon, the delays thus produced may cause a decrease in maternal productivity since Robins adhere to a tight schedule of rearing two or even three broods a season and cannot afford to waste any time.

Rain, moreover, can have even worse effects. Copious downpours may wash away much of the nest's mud and repeatedly force rebuilding efforts. Indeed, even after the nest is completed and stuffed with young, it remains vulnerable to inordinately heavy rains, particularly if it sits on an exposed branch. Too often intense thunderstorms have succeeded in softening a Robin's nest and then, tragically, down tumble babies, cradle and all.

In conclusion, we might note several practices—suggested by the Robin's nesting habits—by which you can encourage a pair of Redbreasts to build in your own backyard. Following these hints, of course, won't guarantee success since suitability for nest-building is not the only characteristic which makes a given locality attractive to Robins. (Food supply, for example, is also important.) Nevertheless, the following suggestions are well worth a try.

A pan of wet clay set out on the lawn is a godsend to a Robin who is just beginning work on the mud layer of her nest. Should the weather be at all dry, she will probably be quick indeed to utilize this unexpected source of plaster. Robins also appreciate string, cotton, and other building materials that are made convenient for them. Pieces of string or yarn, however, should not be more than a foot long. Imprudent Robins have been known to wrap themselves up with string, thereby becoming trapped in a mess that is either fatal or, as the following newspaper article describes, just plain embarrassing:

Fireman Frees Tangled Robin

Waukegan, Ill. (AP)—A high-strung Robin got the Waukegan Fire Department out at dawn today to save his neck. In search of home-building materials, he lit on a fine long piece of string but got himself all tangled up in it. Sam Gordon, a Waukegan merchant, called the Fire Department and a fireman on a ladder truck set the bird free. *(New York Times, 1934)*

Rumor has it that when this poor fellow finally returned to his nest, his blushing face turned as crimson as his breast, and his mate—apparently mistaking him for a flirting Cardinal—indignantly chased him away.

In addition to providing materials, you can create a good nesting site in your yard by erecting a sturdy shelf some five to twenty feet from the ground, preferably beneath a branch or other structure that will afford protection from heavy rains and summer sun. Since Robins are not hole-nesters and would therefore not use a closed birdhouse, the support shelf should be open on at least three sides. A piece of wood six inches wide and eight inches long, perforated with several small drain holes, will be certain to gain Mrs. Robin's grateful approval.

chapter 6

Bringing Up Baby

Stealing quietly along, I came in sight of the male Robin, loudly calling, fluttering his wings, and in evident trouble, though I could not imagine the cause. But looking closely I saw perched on a branch of a cedar-tree a fat, stupid-looking bird, fully as big as the Robin and covered with feathers, but with a speckled breast and no tail to mention. There he sat like a lump of dough, head down in his shoulders and bill sticking almost straight up, and neither the tenderest coaxing nor the loudest scolding moved him in the least. In fact, I thought he was dead till the opera-glass showed that he winked. But stupid and ugly as he looked, he was the darling of the heart in Papa's little red breast.
—Olive Thorne Miller, 1883

Migration, territoriality, courtship, nest-building—these are all fundamental links in the cyclical chain of Robin life. But each is largely without significance, without utility, without import, unless viewed in the context of the eventual rearing of babies. Baby-making, after all, forms one half of the crux of any species' existence, death being the other half. And no matter how terribly awkward in appearance or irritatingly demanding of attention babies may characteristically seem, they just happen to be the stuff of the future.

For Robins, progeny production can be conveniently divided into categories of parental activity corresponding to each of the three major phases of songbird babyhood: the egg, the nestling, and the fledgling. Lacking a more creative approach, we will proceed in that order.

First an Egg

One or two days after her nest is completed, the female Robin begins laying eggs at the rate of one per day, with the morning being her favorite dropping time. Her eggs are usually glossy sky-blue in color ("Robin's-egg blue" has actually served as a stand-ardized hue in our culture), but may occasionally be greenish blue or, rarely, either spotted or entirely white. For some reason, the shells become progressively less glossy from first-laid to last, so that the female's final effort is often quite dull. In similar fashion, her eggs also tend to become progressively smaller across a given set.

Although four eggs is the typical total, three is not an uncommon clutch size, and occasionally five are laid. As many as eight eggs in one nest have been reported several times, but such clutches probably always arise from the joint efforts of two different females, one of whom for some reason does not have a nest of her own. It is conceivable, however, that a single bird might lay up to six eggs. Interestingly, Robins seem to lay more eggs per clutch in the northern parts of their range (for example, New England) than in the southern parts (for example, Georgia), but this tendency is rather slight.

With the onset of egg-laying, Mother Robin is confronted with the problem of when to begin incubation. If she starts with the laying of the first egg, then—since the eggs are laid a day apart from each other—the first-laid egg will obviously hatch one day before the second-laid egg hatches, and two days before the third-laid egg. In that case, considerable discrepancy will exist between the size and strength of the first- and last-hatched youngsters, and the latter will be at a severe and potentially lethal disadvantage in competing with older nestmates for food. From this perspective, it behooves the female to wait until her clutch is complete before beginning incubation (depending on the temperature, fertilized eggs can remain viable for several days before the onset of incubation). And in general, this is exactly what she does.

On the other hand, the cold night air of early spring could easily injure the first-laid egg if it is not protected by an incubating female. To prevent such damage, the female should ideally begin incubating as soon as she lays that first egg. And, lo and behold, Robins do tend to initiate incubation before their clutches are complete when local temperatures drop dangerously low. In other words, although her general predisposition is to begin incubating only after the clutch is complete, wise Mother Robin will start sooner in the face of chilly weather.

With little exception, the monotonous chore of incubation falls upon the responsible, feathered shoulders of the female. It is she who spends the entire night on the nest as well as 60 to 80 percent of the daytime, depending again on the weather: on cold days, somehow sensing that her eggs mustn't lie uncovered for long, she sits more continuously than she does during milder temperatures. Even during warm weather, however, the female is careful to be gone for no more than five or ten minutes during each of the one or two times an hour that she does leave the nest. These brief and perhaps welcomed excursions from her tedious chore, of course, are necessary for obtaining food since, as we noted in Chapter 4, the female's territorial-minded mate seldom feeds her as she incubates. Though relatively constant throughout the incubation period, the mother's "attentiveness" (periods spent on the nest) tends to increase a bit as hatch-time approaches.

One interesting sidelight to the female's incubation duties is the periodic "turning" or rotating of the eggs. In most avian species, the embryos are likely to develop abnormally if they maintain a constant position with respect to the direction of gravity. Anyone who has ever artificially hatched chicks or ducklings, for example, knows that during incubation the eggs must be turned—by either hand or machine—several times daily so that different sides of each shell face upward at different times. Mother Robin must also rotate her eggs, and so every now and then she interrupts her sitting, hops onto the nest's rim, and gently rolls the eggs with her bill.

After twelve or thirteen days of patient warming aided by a special hot-spot on the female's underside (known as a "brood patch"), the eggs begrudgingly begin to yield their precious contents to the outside world. The shells that had shielded out environmental harshness during fragile embryonic development now act like confining prison walls that must be fractured for freedom, and each infant—tooled with a special hard protrusion on its beak (called an "egg tooth")—laboriously chisels away from the inside. Struggling and resting, struggling and resting, the youngster may require an entire day before finally breaking out. Then exhausted, featherless, wet, and blind, the infant fatefully collapses into the next phase of its existence.

Next a Nestling

The physical development of a nestling is nothing less than astounding. Infants who weigh five grams at hatching generally tip the scales at about fifty-five grams a week and a half later—a spectacular increase of 1,000 percent in only ten days. Many other physical changes coincide with these weight gains, of course, and together the developmental processes mirror a miraculous metamorphosis from naked helplessness to something at least approaching feathered autonomy.

Except for a few bits of tufted down, the newly hatched

Robin's most striking features are its painfully pink skin, two huge but closed black eyes, a swollen stomach, a long, skinny neck, and a periodically gaping orange-lined mouth. For at least the first few days, the infant is largely soundless, its body temperature rests at an abnormally low level (about 103°F), and it cannot stand or even sit upright. It can, in fact, raise its head for periods of only a few seconds, during which time it passively accepts anything shoved down its yawning little mouth.

By the sixth day after hatching, however, the nestling has opened its eyes, feather sheaths have appeared above the skin, it can hold its head up for thirty seconds straight, and for the first time the baby can actively grasp objects with its mandibles. By day eight the youngster is feathered everywhere except perhaps on the stomach, its body maintains adult temperatures of around 109°F, it can now sit upright, and its food call during parental presence approaches vociferation. By day ten or eleven the more precocious of the young are capable of leaving the nest, and only their speckled breasts, stubby tails, and smaller size readily distinguish them from adults.

We might briefly note one other interesting change that occurs during a nestling's development—namely, the gradual appearance of the ability to show "fear." In the Robin, as in most animals, fear of novel or potentially threatening objects is initially absent in the neonate; such emotional responses only begin to appear after some period of maturation. The length of this maturational period varies greatly with the particular species, being about twenty-four hours in a newly hatched duckling, a couple of months in an infant monkey, and about six to nine months in a human baby. In Robins, fear first appears between the sixth and tenth day after hatching. Thus, while a two-day-old nestling will show no signs of distress when being handled, a ten-day-old nestling will struggle most violently. What underlies this gradual emergence of fear-ability is not clear, but it is not simply the development of sight since some Robins do not show fear until day ten even though their eyes may have opened on day six.

Throughout the course of all these rapid nestling changes, the parents are constantly tending the infants' various needs. And perhaps nothing reflects the solicitous nature of this parental care better than the occasional survival of a baby who is markedly handicapped in some way or other. One nestling, for example, suffered from a malformed tongue which protruded through the lower mandible and hung like a billygoat's beard in pathetic uselessness. This baby remained fit and fat while being fed by its parents, but upon leaving the nest and meeting difficulty in self-feeding, the youngster grew emaciated under decreasing parental provisions and eventually succumbed. A similar case involved a totally blind nestling who, with diligent parental care, managed to survive to fledglinghood (that is, grew old enough to leave the nest). Quite expectedly, however, the poor youngster soon began blundering into various obstacles and twice even had to be fished from a backyard pool by human passersby. The creature's final fate, though unknown, could not have been a pleasant one; yet the important point is that it had managed to survive as a nestling in the first place.

If infant Robins are to endure their first two-week period of posthatch life, their parents must successfully meet the problems posed by three different nestling needs: the need for food, the need for nest sanitation, and the need for protection against both predators and the elements. Of these three labors, the most exhausting in both time and effort is the provision of food.

Food

Nestlings consume tremendous quantities of food, often amounting to 50 percent more than their own weights within a twelve-hour period. Indeed, one researcher discovered to his supreme stupefaction that a nestling Robin could, within a single day, gulp down some fourteen feet of earthworm! Small wonder the infants grow so fast. And small wonder that baby Robins so frequently starve to death in the care of human foster parents who just don't realize how quickly a nestling's food metabolizes and must be replaced. In any event, the amount of food which the parent Robins collect for their babies over the entire two-week nestling period totals about three pounds. Surprisingly, this amount does not vary significantly with the number of youngsters in the nest; thus members of a two-baby brood get much more nourishment per baby than those in a brood consisting of four or five young.

In futile efforts to stuff their seemingly bottomless babies to the brim, both parents work feverishly from dawn to dusk. Indeed, all day long each adult completes a shuttle between nest and lawn every five or ten minutes, although the mother may occasionally take time off to warm the youngsters by brooding (sitting over) them, an activity she also does throughout the night. Should one of the parents be killed by cat or car during this crucial period, the surviving partner faces a herculean though not impossible task in nourishing the ravenous infants. In those cases where the nestlings are still quite young (and hence unfeathered), the mother would have a better chance of successfully rearing the babies alone since the father would be unlikely to brood them sufficiently to avoid lethal chilling, especially during the night. One Robin widower in Michigan, however, benefited from human intervention in the form of an ice-fisherman's pocket-warmer that was securely fitted into the nest; his babies thus nice and warm, the male managed to feed and finally fledge two nestlings by himself.

In another case of one-parent rearing, a widowed mother raised her young despite a wing injury that precluded flight. Fortunately, since her nest rested on the first limb of a leaning tree, she could travel from ground to young by hopping, albeit with great effort, up the Tower of Pisa trunk. *Labor omnia vincit,* you might say if you spoke Latin. Happily, the mother's wing healed just as her nestlings fledged.

The type of food that the parents give their nestlings consists primarily of animal matter, for although Robins are quite fond of fruits, most berries do not ripen until too late in the nesting season. In addition to earthworms, the babies are fed grubs, spiders, caterpillars, grasshoppers, beetles, and a host of other insects. While many of these animals are not antagonists of humanity, and some are indeed beneficial, a great number are noxious. And considering that a single pair of Robins harvests three pounds of buggy crop in raising each of their two or three broods per summer, we can well appreciate the invaluable contribution that the species as a whole makes toward keeping insect populations in check. Robins, together with their fellow songbirds, truly constitute essential ballast in the balance of Nature.

The Mechanics of Feeding. Although the parents may initially feed their newly hatched nestlings by regurgitating food that has already been partly digested, they soon deliver whole worms and insects into the nestlings' gaping mouths. Seeming perhaps a rather simple process, parental feeding of the young instead represents a complex interchange of numerous behavioral signals.

During the initial six-day period of blindness, for example, the infants reflexively respond to any jiggle of the nest (such as is caused by the parents when they land) with an immediate and vigorous stretch of the neck, an exigent opening of the mouth, and a series of clamorous calls that continue until food is received. Later, after their eyes have opened, the young expectantly emit this begging behavior upon the mere sight of their approaching but still-airborne parents. Begging may be even further elicited by a "dinner is served" call which the parents frequently emit as they arrive.

Just as the visible approach, jiggling landing, and dinnertime calls of the parents initiate "begs" from the babies, these begs in turn have a decided effect on parental behavior. In general, the tiny head held highest and the gaping mouth spread widest wins the worm. The goods are delivered with a deep thrust of the parent's bill down into the bright orange-lined throat of the baby. This bright inner color of a nestling's mouth may be an additional sort of stimulation that encourages feeding by the parent; in other words, an orange gaping mouth may mechanically elicit bill-thrusting by Robin parents in much the same way that a red breast seems to reflexively elicit aggression.

But the most important point to be deduced from the above discussion is that the parents—rather than following a strict rotational system in which each baby must await its turn—instead tend to feed the nestling who begs the most vigorously, even if that happens to be the same youngster who received food on the immediately preceding visit. Less vigorous nestmates, meanwhile, must await another parental trip. Clearly, this type of procedure favors the feeding of a brood's biggest and strongest babies at the expense of any weakling who cannot lift its head as high. As a result, precious and hard-got nourishment is not wasted among infants who, perhaps because of some inborn defect that saps their strength, are destined to meet an early death regardless of parental care.

If, on the other hand, all the babies are healthy and strong, no single one among them will manage to grab all of the handouts. This is because the magnitude of the begging behavior gradually declines as a baby grows less hungry. Thus, once a given youngster has obtained a meal, its begging upon the parents' next visit will tend to be less intense than that of its still-hungry nestmates, who will consequently be fed their due.

In summary, then, the formidable task of keeping a nestful of baby Robins well-nourished involves an intricate exchange of behavioral signals between parents and infants. The parents, by their food calls, their landing on the nest, and their visible approach, elicit begging from the nestlings. In turn, this begging behavior—including neck stretching, mouth gaping (which displays the orange-lined throat), and begging calls—stimulates the parents to thrust into the inviting mouths whatever food they are carrying. The automatic and reflexive nature of this parental thrusting, by the way, is blatantly revealed by the fact that even after dispensing a load of food, a parent sometimes rethrusts its now-empty bill down a baby's throat if the greedy infant continues to beg.

Sanitation

The enormous appetite of a baby Robin quite naturally leads to a substantial solid waste problem. Indeed, a nestling defecates nearly as frequently as it eats. This presents a serious problem. Were Robins unable or disinclined to keep their nests immaculate, harmful bacteria, parasites, and flies would be constant menaces to the young, not to mention the dreadful threat of gradual suffocation. So the parents, most especially the mother, always practice scrupulous sanitation habits and never permit any excrement to remain in the nest for long.

The excrement itself is voided by the babies in neat white self-contained "fecal sacs." The parents may actually eat these sacs with no ill aftereffects, and indeed perhaps with a little nourishment. Or they may carry the sacs away after each visit so that an efficient regimen of food-delivery and waste-evacuation characterizes each nest trip. In this case, the sacs will be ferried some distance away from the nest rather than simply toileted over its edge, since this latter practice would furnish a potential nest-location clue for any predator who spotted the white splashes on the ground below.

The parents' meticulousness also extends to other potentially pathogenetic material in the nest as well. Should one of the

youngsters die, for example, the mother will remove its body with sorrowed promptness. Occasionally in her rush to cleanse the cradle, she may toss out something of value. Once a Robin dropped a sizable package into a camping area as she flew overhead; upon inspection, the parcel proved to be a stunned nestling with a long piece of liver protruding from its bill. Apparently the mother—having found the liver in nearby trash— attempted to give the lengthy meal to her infant. The offering was, however, more than the youngster could handle, and at her next visit the mother plucked up the loose unswallowed end with intent to discard it, without at all realizing that she was throwing out her baby with the bath.

Protection

As threats to life, both predators and adverse weather are far more formidable after the young hatch, as compared to before. Within their eggshells, Robin embryos are assured the nearly continuous presence of their mother who discreetly incubates with quiet inconspicuousness. Squirrels, Crows, Blue Jays, and other potential enemies will have trouble first in locating the nest, and then in overcoming the valiant defenses of the mother as well as her mate, who is quickly summoned to the site by the female's cries of alarm. Weatherwise, of course, the eggs are almost always shielded by the sitting female from the harshness of too much heat, too much cold, or too much rain. All of this sharply contrasts with the situation of hatched Robins. Now, a bustle of activity envelops the nest, with both parents constantly coming and going as they strive to keep three or four noisy babies well fed. Obviously, such activity can easily attract the attention of predators; in addition, the chances that the young will be unprotected from either predators or harsh weather are increased.

Without doubt, parental presence means everything to Robin nestlings. Often courageous, Robin parents enjoy a relatively large size (as songbirds go) and corresponding strength, and so are capable of powerful defensive attack when their babies are threatened. Usually, a squirrel or Crow who approaches the nest is quickly deterred by a determinedly diving parent, and the short skirmish seldom necessitates the shedding of blood. Sometimes, however, real injury results. In one report, a female Robin killed a large Steller's Jay who persisted in menacing her nest; then both she and her mate proceeded to batter the Jay's corpse with unassuaged vengeance.

Even humans—enormous creatures that we are—risk a quick, screaming, blow to the forehead should we venture too close to a nestful of young. When one adds the further consideration that the calls of an alarmed parent bring not only his or her mate to the scene but often all other Robins within earshot as well—each of whom is ready and eager to join in any justified fray—one can appreciate how safe Robin nestlings really are in the presence of their parents.

Parental presence is also important in protecting nestlings against cool nights, hot suns, and strong storms. After her young have hatched, the mother continues to spend each night on the nest to brood the infants with her warmth through the algid darkness. The daytime may also be too cool, especially during early spring, and this becomes particularly dangerous since the mother is now compelled to help her mate find food for the nestlings and thus is hard-pressed for brooding time.

A much greater threat during the daytime, however, is the intense heat of the summer sun, particularly if the mother has unwisely built her nest at an unshaded site. Very young nestlings will die within fifteen minutes if they are exposed to blistering heat without the shady protection of a brooding mother. On really hot days, the parents may repeatedly fly to a nearby stream or birdbath to fill their bills with cool water for their broiling babies. Nestlings, of course, are much more susceptible to injury from either heat or chill during the first few days after hatching, before insulating feathers have covered their bodies.

Even if the nights and days are moderate in temperature, nestling Robins need motherly protection during rainstorms. To be sure, the youngsters are quite capable of gripping the lining of their nest with surprising strength and are not so easily storm-swept from their little haven; indeed, tenacious nestlings have been known to cling to their nest even after the whole structure has been flung to the ground. Nevertheless, baby birds do need shelter from the rain itself, again especially if they are un-feathered. In one particularly picturesque description of Robins shielding their young during a sudden summer downpour, an admiring observer wrote how a female and her mate

> perched on opposite sides of the nest, breasts pressed together and heads crossed by each other, their bodies and wings thus sheltering the young like a pitched roof, while the rain ran harmlessly off on both sides. (Forbush, 1929)

The singular sight of such selfless parental parasols must have been heart-warming indeed.

At Last, a Fledgling

By the time they are ten days old, Robin nestlings are restlessly active throughout the day. In contrast to the passive between-meal dozing so characteristic of their earlier behavior, they now preen their feathers with persistence and stretch their wings with regularity. As they continually test their newly acquired growth, the three or four fidgety infants almost crowd their tiny nest to overflowing. And perhaps spurred by lack of elbow room as much as anything, the young birds begin to fledge.

Although the proper time for departing the nest is about thirteen days after hatching, the babies often leave prematurely, especially if the nest is disturbed in any way. A person merely wandering too close, for example, can ignite a flapping explosion of plump and chirping cannonballs that scatter in every direction; if this early exodus is more than two or three days ahead of schedule, the youngsters are unlikely to survive. Under less pressing circumstances, the young normally leave their nest one at a time.

But whether fledging occurs under pressured duress or in the gradually emerging face of inevitability, no part of Robin life is as exciting, dramatic, climactic, or utterly clumsy as when a young bird finally breaks away from the nest. With mottled breast and stumpy tail, he dares to do something he's never done before—he dares to fly! Well, almost. Actually, it's more like a fluttering, sputtering descent.

Like a hesitant swimmer debating between abrupt entrance or gradual submergence into an icy pool, the youngster squats on the edge of his nest or along a perch he's boldly hopped onto, and looks doubtfully down at the ground which must seem so far below. Then, with a little coaxing from his parents, encouraged by their calls or enticed with some tasty tidbit, he hops into the air and instinctively flaps with all his might. Still he loses altitude and soon kerplunks on the lawn below, for he cannot after all really fly. He's been fooled, he's been tricked, he's been duped; he is a bird, yet cannot fly. "Am I a lousy penguin?" he asks himself, perhaps.

Though unable—as they will be for the first few days—to sustain horizontal flight, fledglings can sputter diagonally twenty or thirty feet depending on the perch height from which they take off. Nevertheless, it is probably just as well that Robin nests are usually built quite low. But though safe from injuries of impact, fledglings always face the nagging prospect that their first "flight" may inadvertently plop them into some unfortunate situation. Since Robin nests often overhang streams or ponds, for example, the steerless youngsters occasionally wind up treading water on their maiden voyage. Imperiled by finny demons of the deep (not to mention drowning), the buoyant babies usually manage to flap across the water's surface toward the horrified calls of their parents onshore. Once safely beached, the waterlogged infants sit panting, dogshaking, and no doubt wondering whether their overcrowded nest was really so bad after all.

Once the excitement of their first flight is behind them, most fledglings never return to the nest even though they remain in their parents' territory for quite a while. Initially crouching in nestling fashion, the youngsters soon begin to stand erect in the proud manner of the independent adults. But independent they are not as yet, nor will they be for nearly two weeks after leaving the nest. Carefully tended by both parents for a day or so, the young birds are soon left entirely in the tutelage of the father. The mother, meanwhile, departs to build a new nest, lay new eggs, and hatch new nestlings. Thus as soon as the first brood's two-week fledgling period is complete, the father must hurry back to his mate and help raise another batch of newly hatched babies.

Despite plenty of paternal protection, fledgling life is a pretty precarious period for Robins, especially during the first week. And small wonder since the young birds fly only poorly, advertise their location through frequent food calls, and are often still slow to recognize potential danger. Through warning calls that send the fledglings hopping for cover, the ever-anxious fathers manage to handle many problems that arise. But occasionally the youngsters blunder into unusual predicaments that require more ingenious solutions, as the following story attests:

> Madison, Wisc. Pedestrians were placing bets on a parent Robin here, when it finally accomplished the task of freeing a young Robin which had slipped through a sidewalk grating in the business district. Lured by a fat worm waved by the parent, the little Robin made a great effort and was free. *(New York Times,* 1934)

When not calling for food from the bushes or staring dumbly into the playful face of a large tail-wagging dog (or less fortunately, into the hungry eyes of a stalking cat), the fledglings hop around the lawn in the artful footsteps of their foraging father. Trailing a few yards behind, the babies bounce up to their parent as soon as the latter has procured some juicy morsel; then squatting, quivering their wings, calling plaintively, and gaping their mouths, the youngsters are fed in true nestling tradition. Gradually over the two-week term of post-nestling education, the fledglings find increasingly more food on their own. At first pecking randomly at the ground, the birds soon learn through trial and error to discriminate leaves and twigs from worms and beetles, although for a while many of the latter simply wiggle and waddle leisurely away from the clumsy hunters. As time passes, the father may try to hasten his offspring's independence by ignoring more and more of their "feed me!" demands; but if inattention doesn't work and he finally loses forbearance, the parent may resort to more immoderate action. One pop, for example,

> apparently became impatient with the importunities of a helpless fluttering young one almost as large as himself, and seizing a piece of cotton that had lodged in a bush, stuffed it into the mouth of the youngster to keep it quiet. (Forbush, 1929)

Even after "weaning" is complete and the now-flying youngsters can find food for themselves, they often linger in their parents' territory for another week or so before eventually dispersing outward. Though the rate of this dispersion varies from youngster to youngster—with some clinging to parental aprons much longer than others—the outward progress in general is rather slow. Indeed, nearly 60 percent of the young are still within half a mile of their birthplace some two months after leaving the nest. One factor affecting their dispersal, however, is the pattern and extent of cover-providing foliage occurring in immediately outlying regions; dispersion is more rapid in the absence of suitable cover, since then the young birds must "hop over" wide open spaces before temporarily settling down. As they move out from their origins, the young often congregate in considerable numbers at particularly good feeding areas, such as ripening fruit patches. The resulting flocks, in which young Robins may outnumber adults by ten to one, remain intact only so long as the food supply lasts.

In conclusion, we might characterize fledglinghood as an exciting period of Robin life, a period in which young birds progress through a gauntlet of adolescent dangers as they journey from helpless newborns to self-reliant adults. It is a frantic period marked by fretful fathers who—whether scouring the lawn for worms and grubs or flitting through branches to warn and scold—do their darndest to guide inexperienced offspring through teenage traumas. And finally, when all lessons are learned and all tests passed, and the young birds can fend for themselves, fledglinghood climaxes a long series of wonderful natural events, events that began even before the deliberating female first selected a site for her muddy, grass-lined nest.

Not Just a Family Affair

Although the rearing of young is typically a private project, a task that each pair of Robins usually undertake and complete entirely by themselves, other birds may occasionally contribute to the effort. Being territorial, of course, the parents seldom allow other Redbreasts near enough to the nest to participate in the care of eggs or nestlings. During the fledgling stage, however, nonparent Robins can more readily become involved since the youngsters may then wander out of their parents' territory and into that of their neighbors; moreover, even when the bush-hiding babies do remain near their own nest, their loudly insistent food cries often entice nearby adults—whose own young may still be but eggs—to trespass with foody appeasements. Thus numerous instances have been reported of Robin foster parents feeding, protecting and in general adopting strange fledglings who may or may not have been separated from their own parents.

Such incidents, of course, clearly demonstrate the powerful ability of a young Robin to arouse, through its own infantile behavior, the parental instincts of unrelated adults. Interestingly, the adults don't even have to be other Robins, for cooperative parenthood can transgress interspecies boundaries as well. To cite but a few examples: a Mourning Dove once added her eggs to those in a Robin's nest, and then took turns incubating with the mother Redbreast; Song Sparrows have been known to not only feed baby Robins but to clean their nest as well; Bluebirds once defended a fledgling Robin from Blue Jay attack; and two Cardinals reportedly dive-bombed a cat who held a fledgling Robin in his mouth (under the awesome onslaught, the feline freed the frightened but otherwise unharmed youngster).

In another, more prolonged instance of Cardinal-Robin teamwork, pairs of both species began building their nests on the same tree in Reynoldsburg, Ohio. After a storm destroyed the Cardinals' nest, however, the Redbirds not only helped their neighbors complete their nest, but even added their eggs to those of the Robins in the hybrid structure. With the two mothers incubating in shifts and the fathers getting along equally well, one egg of each species eventually hatched. The four parents then worked in harmony to nourish the step-siblings—with the Redbreasts dispensing worms *in toto,* and the Redcrests regurgitating bugs *au jus.*

In short, then, numerous birds have been known to contribute to nearly every possible phase of Robin familyhood—including nest construction, egg-laying and incubation, nestling-feeding and sanitation, and fledgling protection. Naturally, there have also been complementary cases where Robins have played the benevolent role of benefactor by helping to raise non-Robin babies. Perhaps the most unusual instance of such Robin goodwill involved a male who adopted a motherless baby chick. Now, chicks—unlike baby Robins—are well developed when they hatch; within mere hours they are quite capable of pecking the ground for food, and do not like having it crammed into their mouths the way Robin nestlings do. Thus whenever the well-intentioned Redbreast tried to give the fluffy youngster a worm via normal Robin procedures (down the throat), the chick steadfastly refused the meal. Just as the male was about to abandon his seemingly futile efforts, however, he happened to drop the worm on the ground, whereupon the baby gobbled up the juicy tidbit quite promptly. This fortuitous fumble apparently bridged the communication gap between these distantly related birds, because the Robin then proceeded to toss worms and bugs at the feet of the hungry and thereafter receptive chick.

Before closing the present topic, we might note that some birds have other than honorable intentions when they participate in the Robin's family chores. Once, for example, an English Sparrow developed the habit of perching on the edge of a Robin's nest whenever one of the parents appeared with an insect for the young; then, as the parent attempted to feed its nestlings, the sneaky Sparrow would snatch up the morsel instead. Fortunately, though this felony occurred frequently during the two-week nestling period, the persevering parents nevertheless managed to get sufficient nourishment to their victimized babies.

An interloper who more commonly threatens to take undue advantage of the Robin's parental instincts is the Cowbird. The female Cowbird apparently does not care for the trials and tribulations of motherhood, for she always lays her egg in an unguarded nest of another species with the hope that it will be incubated, hatched, and reared by the foster parents when they return. Robins, luckily, only rarely accept a Cowbird's egg in the first place; more often they impatiently puncture the uninvited ovum or indignantly eject it from the nest. A Robin's annoyance at the Cowbird's deed will be even more manifest should the freeloading culprit be caught in the insidious act.

In one reported case, for instance, a Cowbird landed on a Robin's nest right after the incubating female had flown out of sight. When the Robin returned in time to interrupt the Cowbird's deposition, however, she promptly attacked the latter with vengeful viciousness. Easily outweighing the intruder, the Redbreast nastily knocked the Cowbird to the ground and then spitefully struck her with wing and beak. After a full minute of such flogging the Cowbird finally made her escape, though leaving blood-stained spots and a warm egg on the grass behind her. In this classic clash of maternal instincts, Robinhood had won.

A final frequent participant in the Robin's family affairs is the well-intentioned human who, coming upon an unattended nestful of babies or perhaps some solitary fledgling, assumes the role of the apparently lost parents. In most cases this is a mistake, for hand-rearing baby songbirds is an extremely difficult endeavor which often ends in failure. Likely as not, moreover, the parents were only temporarily absent when their offspring were "rescued." Thus, unless circumstances clearly indicate otherwise, one should always presume that Robin youngsters—no matter how abandoned they appear to be—are in fact receiving proper parental care. (Fledglings in particular, by the way, possess a special knack for appearing woefully alone and abandoned even when they are not; desolation is, in fact, a guise they seem to rehearse.) Accordingly, Robin youngsters in general should not be disturbed, and if they are inadvertently handled (for example, by children), they should be promptly returned to wherever they were first found.

Occasionally, however, baby birds are obviously injured or

orphaned, and human intervention offers their only chance for survival. If the babies are nestlings only a few days old, they will require considerable heat since newly hatched songbirds are initially unable to regulate their own body temperatures. Equally important, they must be fed quite often—as much as every ten to twenty minutes from dawn to dusk. Their diet should be varied and of a high-protein content; one recommended mixture includes freshly killed bugs (or, perhaps, bits of mealworm), wheat germ, turkey starter, gelatin, egg yolk (hard-boiled), dog food, applesauce, cottage cheese, strained carrots, and small amounts of cod liver oil and human baby vitamins. Little or no water should be given. Of course, older nestlings and fledglings— who can maintain their body temperatures and are able to consume much more food at each feeding—are far easier to nurse, and much more likely to survive under human care.

chapter 7

Death's Ruthless Race

At twenty, the Condor who had soared nearly a half a million miles over his mountainous range was tired. He had lived seven thousand and three hundred days, he had pressed himself to the bodies of two females, one of them his own offspring, and had produced a desperately needed crop of successful chicks. He was immortal. He had known peace, and he had known fear. He had cheated death more times than we can know and had thereby protected his potential, keeping it from harm until it was used up. His had been a successful life and he had lived it in the sun.

—Roger Caras, 1970

Right now in Southern California, a priceless piece of American heritage is being swept along the river of extinction and into the gulf of oblivion. Pushed into the deadly waters by obscenities of human self-centeredness, the magnificent California Condor is finding the unnatural pressures far different from the air currents that his nine-foot wingspan was meant to ride, and he is drowning.

In 1947, after years of declining numbers brought on by our thoughtless land-use, our greedy egg-collecting, our inadvertent and thus stupid poisoning, and our outright shooting, only about sixty California Condors remained alive on this planet. By 1966 there were only fifty. Even now, with heavy protection and ample food supplies, this living relic—a contemporary of the legendary saber-toothed tiger—is barely able to hold his own against the downsweeping current, much less flounder to safety onshore. Why, now given the chance, can't the species recover? Why can't the Condor quickly replenish his decimated population and soar once again far above the waters that threaten him?

Unhappily, the answer lies largely within the Condor's own physiology: his reproductive potential is nothing more than meager. Although he can expect to live some twenty years, a baby Condor takes five whole years of painstaking development before breeding for the first time. And even then the female lays only one egg every other year! Contrast these statistics with those of the American Robin who—with a potential lifespan of ten or twelve years—can breed a year after hatching and then lays about four eggs, two or three times a nesting season. There is no comparison.

A given pair of Condors can at most fledge fewer than ten babies in their lifetime; a pair of Robins can fledge close to a hundred. But the real biological power of the Robin is not fully appreciated until one takes into account the potential breeding by a given pair's own young in subsequent years. Suppose, for example, one pair annually fledges two broods of four young each, and that all the young survive and reproduce at the same rate. Assuming no mortality, the original pair of Robins will have 19.5 million descendants by the end of their ten-year life-span! (Comparable calculations for the Condor show a potential of only thirty descendants during a given pair's lifetime.) At the end of a mere thirty years, the original pair of Robins would have 1.2 billion trillion descendants! That's quite a few Robins. So many, in fact, that according to the computations of one scientist, only one out of every one hundred fifty thousand of these birds would fit on the entire surface of the earth if they were to stand shoulder to shoulder.

The point of these hypothetical statistics is the simple but important fact that if humanity's arrogance should ever shove the American Robin into the same river that the California Condor now finds itself, the Robin would at least have the breeding potential to make a biological comeback with veritable motor-boat speed. (This assumes, of course, that the species could be protected from its enemies and that enough Robins were still alive to locate mates during the breeding season.)

What's that you now say? You wonder why, given such great breeding potential, Robins do not overrun our planet? Why doesn't each redbreasted pair have almost 20 million descendants by the end of their lifetime? The answer is as easy as its implications are profound: hardly any Robins survive long in Nature. Though Robins have a natural longevity potential of ten years (in captivity, they may live close to twenty!), their average actual lifespan has been estimated at less than one-and-a-half years.

Consider these staggering statistics of Robin mortality: of every hundred eggs laid each year, at least thirty never survive to hatch; and of the seventy nestlings that do hatch, thirty die before fledging. In other words, for every 100 Robin eggs, only forty birds live to leave the nest! The other sixty are obliterated during their first three-and-a-half weeks of existence. How many Robins live as long as one year? About seven out of a hundred. How many live three years? One or two, out of a hundred. How many Robins live five years? Only about one out of every four hundred—that's how many!

Death. Death pursues every Robin, from embryo to nestling to fledgling to adult. In this classic race of survival, propagation waits at the finish-line but precious few contestants get there in time. Precious few Robins live to breed even once, much less repeatedly. That's why our planet is not overrun. In a moment, we'll see the many ways death can win this ruthless race. But first, there's an interesting point to be made.

Many people discourage, or even condemn, the rearing in captivity of a "wild" animal. They say a wild animal is meant to be free. But what price freedom? With conscientious care, pet Robins can live ten years; indeed, one methuselahn Redbreast lived a full seventeen years under a kind lady's care, and "sung as well and looked as sprightly at that age as ever" but alas, finally fell into the fatal fangs of a cat. A Robin free in Nature, on the other hand, will most likely never see his first birthday.

Are Robins "happier" in Nature than out of it? I doubt it. Oh perhaps when sun shines, worms wiggle, and berries ripen. But what about when lightning cracks, cold wind howls, and rain plummets down? And what about the care and affection that a human can share with a pet? The ornithological literature is sprinkled with heart-warming reports of wild birds kept as pets, which appeared to be perfectly contented and satisfied with their circumstances. Some animals, to be sure—because of innate disposition, or age, or previous experience—cannot be satisfactorily brought into one's home. They mope and withdraw, they become irritable and vicious, or they just plain die. But such is not a universal outcome of captivity. Robins reared as nestlings frequently seem to adapt to the situation, to enjoy their human companions, and to live long full lives if properly cared for.

All of this is not to advocate widespread and systematic removal of Robins from Nature for confinement in cages. There are, in fact, federal laws prohibiting most sorts of songbird captivity. But in the context of relative longevity, the propriety of humans rearing undomesticated animals deserves at least some thoughtful revaluation.

Now, let's look at some of the many causes of Robin

mortality. These causes are of two basic categories: natural and human-related.

Natural Causes of Death

Natural causes of death among Robins include disease, weather, and predators. Of what consequences disease is to the Robin population is difficult to assess; probably it is minimal, at least as a direct cause of death. Most territorial species—as opposed to those who live in herds or colonies—are fairly resistant to large-scale spread of contagious diseases by virtue of the self-imposed spacing of their population. Robins, despite their strong territoriality during the breeding season, would seem to forfeit this disease-limiting advantage by their daily nighttime roosting in tight flocks (see Chapter 10). Still, if any serious epidemics have ever plagued Robins, it's as yet gone unnoticed by birdwatchers.

With Robins—and this is true of many other wild animals as well—disease is probably much more often a contributing cause of death than it is the sole cause. Sickly Robins are more apt to succumb to harsh weather or be caught by predators than are healthy Robins. This is of course one of the indispensable contributions that a predator makes to the welfare of the species upon which it preys—the quick removal of diseased individuals who might otherwise spread their affliction to conspecifics. Thus it is not only the raptor-lover who says, "Save the hawk, save the owl." It is the Robin-lover as well!

Unlike disease, weather can often be an obvious, even spectacular cause of Robin death. As pointed out in Chapter 6, babies as well as eggs can be thunderstormed from a nest, doomed to lie dying in the mud below with only the plaintive calls of their helpless parents to soothe them in that final sleep. More violent weather can kill adults almost as easily. Once after a midnight storm on Long Island, thirty-six dead Robins were found on a single acre where they had been devastated while roosting the night before. One July, a tornado hit Portsmouth, Iowa, and left seventy-one Robins scattered over two acres like so many russet autumn leaves. Sometimes following these local catastrophes, Robins are completely eliminated from the whole area for the entire season. Other times, the void is quickly filled by an influx of birds from nearby localities that happened to escape the brunt of the storm. It should also be noted that despite their otherwise hardy character, Robins seem to be felled more easily than some other birds; scrappy English Sparrows and hole-nesting Starlings usually fare much better in harsh weather.

As far as natural predators go, the Robin's primary enemies include cats, dogs, squirrels, Crows, Jays, owls, and hawks. Cats and dogs are most dangerous to young Robins, those who have just fledged, still fly poorly, and spend a lot of time on the ground and in low-lying bushes. Crows, Jays and squirrels attack even younger Robins—those still in the nest—as well as the Robin's eggs. When parent Robins find any of these nest-robbers near their young, they scold and dive-bomb until they drive the intruder away. Sometimes, however, the crime is committed before the thieves can be routed.

The diurnal hawks and the nocturnal owls prey upon young and old Robins alike. Among the winged predators caught in the act of eating Robins are Cooper's Hawks, Goshawks, Sparrow Hawks, Marsh Hawks, Pigeon Hawks, Peregrine Falcons, Gyrfalcons, Horned Owls, Barred Owls, Screech Owls, and Snowy Owls (the latter occasionally coming as far south as New England). Robins may be a bit more susceptible to hawking than shier songbirds who are more reluctant to fly across open spaces where the great birds of prey can snatch them. Owls, being largely nighttime hunters, would probably not get many Robins were it not for the Robin's propensity for being an early riser, early enough to cross paths with many an owl who is just about to retire for the day.

Frequently Robins are fed to baby owls and hawks. Observation of twelve different nests of Cooper's Hawks in Ithaca, New York, once revealed that the forty-two youngsters residing therein were fed seventy-nine Robins before they fledged. Yet despite the fact that owls and hawks like to serve them as baby food, insolent Robins have been known to nest right next door to these breeding raptors, and moreover with a surprisingly reliable degree of safety. Why? Because many birds of prey try to avoid disturbances (such as those caused in the capture of protesting Robins) in the immediate vicinity of their own nest.

Should the opportunity arise, Robins will bravely show antagonism toward those birds who prey upon them. Should a few Redbreasts discover an owl at his daytime perch, they may dive-bomb (without making contact) and scream at him for the better part of an hour. This practice, common among small birds, is known as "mobbing." A Robin's mobbing cry will attract not only all the other Robins in the neighborhood but other species as well, and soon dozens of songbirds will be loudly venting anger toward their hated foe. Most interestingly, the owl will not retaliate but merely endure the insults or, should patience fail him, fly off to find another, more secluded spot to roost.

Robins will also fly at a hawk on the wing, should he be seen carrying away one of their species in his talons. If the killer is a small bird—as is the Sparrow Hawk, who only weighs 120 grams compared to the Robin's 80—the raptor may have considerable difficulty outmaneuvering his screaming pursuers as he labors with his prey. As in owl-mobbing, numerous species of songbird may join forces in harassing a hawk caught red-taloned. Kingbirds have been seen chasing a Cooper's Hawk who had just snatched a baby Robin from its nest, and Robins have been known to dive at a Sparrow Hawk who was menacing the nest of a House Sparrow.

In addition to the above major predators, there are a few minor ones who sometimes manage to catch a Robin or two.

Snapping turtles, believe it or not, have been known to eat Robins, albeit ever so rarely. In fact it is only circumstantial evidence—and not eyewitness report—that earns this fiercesome pond predator a paragraph in our book. One summer a surprised woman in Nashville, Tennessee, found bird feathers (including those of Robins) floating in her backyard lily-pond. The killer's identity remained a mystery even after flour was spread on the rocks around the pool, for this ploy only revealed the tracks of the victims as they strolled into the shallow waters to bathe and drink. Surmising that the predator was aquatic, the detective drained the pool and discovered a slightly suspicious pair of grinning snappers who were thereupon urged to vacate the premises. After that, Robin casualties ceased and the case was closed.

Other Robin enemies have been less covert in their deeds. Snakes sometimes procure adult Robins, although usually only after the victims show regrettably poor judgment. More than one Robin has been strangled by a small snake whose tail only moments before had appeared to be a deliciously fat worm lying seductively in the grass. Bigger snakes sometimes attack Robin nests in the trees. Once in Franklin, Massachusetts, a woman and her husband were drawn to the dramatic scene of a screaming Father Robin who was "fluttering directly over a snake's head and making every possible effort to drive him away" from an egg-filled nest. In a clear example of well-intentioned but irrationally extreme human intervention, the callous couple—instead of merely removing the snake from the vicinity—axed the poor serpent because "we felt that positive proof of the lawlessness of this one justified his death." Lawlessness? Whose laws, I wonder.

But perhaps the most unusual case of predation upon Robins—besides the snapping turtle incident—occurred in Anahuac, Texas, during the particularly cold winter of 1894. Frequent snows had cut off food supplies from many visiting migrants, among them flocks of Rusty Blackbirds. These birds soon took to attacking Robins who had gathered to feed on a certain field that had been thawed by a warm artesian well. Though presumably novices at avian predation, the blackbirds slaughtered dozens of Robins like practiced experts. After making a kill, the attackers ate only the victim's brain, leaving the body itself untouched.

Human-Related Mortality

Many instances of Robin mortality are unavoidable accidents, minimum prices that Robins pay for living so close to humans. Cars, for example, continually take a set percentage of our wildlife, and Robins are not immune to fatal collisions. In fact, since Robins tend to skim along the ground during the initial part of their flights from lawn to tree, they may be a little more vulnerable to car-colliding than other birds who ascend more quickly after takeoff.

We have already mentioned that nest-building Robins sometimes tangle themselves in string, and such predicaments can be fatal if the bird cannot free herself. Robins can apparently even mistake string for a worm; one bird ate twenty inches of twine and then died when it obstructed the intestinal tract. Death has also overtaken Robins through means of invisible window panes, shocking high tension wires, and one-chance-in-a-million beanings by meteoric golfballs. But such misfortunes are rare accidents, hardly significant factors in their effects on the Robin population. Of more important consequence are fatalities arising from human use of pesticides, human defense of cultivated crops, and historically, human use of Robins themselves as food.

Pesticidal Poisoning

Robins have often inadvertently been killed in our chemical attacks on a variety of different enemies, such as mosquitoes, aphids, and Japanese beetles. But most often and dramatically they have been cast in the role of innocent-but-injured bystanders in our battles against Dutch elm disease. This disease involves a fungus that is carried by bark beetles, who thereby spread the affliction from elm to elm. Across widespread regions of the United States, the malady has rendered groves of beautiful trees into cemeteries of ugly skeletons. In the past, our efforts to save these trees have usually centered on smothering the bark beetles with large quantities of DDT (dichloro-diphenyl-trichloro-ethane), an unselectively lethal chemical that persists in the environment for an unfortunately long time.

Wherever DDT has been used to combat Dutch elm disease, a deadly cycle has ensued whereby the potent pesticide permeates from one ecological plane to the next, with increasing concentrations of the chemical accumulating at each step. First, leaves sprayed with DDT in either the spring or summer fall in autumn to the ground where, as litter, they are munched over by earthworms. Considerable chemical concentration occurs at this level: DDT that appeared as only 5 parts per million (ppm) in the soil may increase to 30 ppm in the bodies of worms. In other words, as earthworms eat soil, the DDT—rather than passing through and out—instead accumulates in the annelids.

The process then proceeds to some earthworm predator, such as our Robin. By eating DDT-packed worms, Robins thereby concentrate the baneful brew in their own bodies until a fatal level is reached (from 60 to 150 ppm in brain tissue). Declines in Robin numbers of as much as 90 percent have been reported from many heavily sprayed localities. Even at sublethal concentrations, however, DDT may completely negate a Robin's reproductive ability (that is, induce sterility). This obviously is just as deadly a condition for the life of the species as the actual death of the individual would have been.

What's more, these poisoned but surviving Robins may be

preyed upon by animals higher up on the food chain—hawks and owls, for example—and then these predators will die when the chemical becomes too concentrated in their bodies. And of course even dead Robins can pass on the terrible toxin since their contaminated corpses may be discovered by curious cats or ravenous raccoons. Without doubt, DDT is awesome in its sphere of potential influence.

Millions and millions of elms have been sprayed in the United States, and in the process, millions and millions of birds from more than a hundred different species have been fatally poisoned. Groundfeeders like our Robin are particularly vulnerable to this plight—indeed, Robins may account for as much as 50 percent of such avian mortality—and with little doubt the losses of Redbreasts alone have climbed well into the millions, including both adults and unrealized young. Accurate figures for specific localities are hard to come by, but some of the most detailed information comes from Michigan State University where initial studies were followed up in successive years.

In 1954 approximately 185 pairs of Robins, or about one pair per acre, lived on a section of MSU's East Lansing campus. By 1958, after a series of intense DDT programs to fight Dutch elm disease, only one or two pairs remained. The depleted Robin ranks were partially replenished in the spring of 1959 when ten new pairs came on campus to breed, but Robins still continued to die. In fact, by the end of that summer as many as fifty deaths were recorded by campus researchers.

How could fifty Robins die in an area that was initially populated by only ten pairs? Apparently, as campus Robins succumbed to the poison, other birds from nearby areas moved in to fill the void. Thus total Robin losses from DDT included not only the original breeding population but replacement populations as well. More generally it seems likely that DDT, when used at a given locality, affects many more Robins than simply those who are initially living at that locality. Another related and equally important point is that even though Robins may appear to survive within an area that has been sprayed with DDT, many deaths could nevertheless have occurred since replacements often cover up attrition in the original birds.

As mentioned earlier, DDT is a persistent chemical. Indeed, ten years after an application, the ground may still hold 10 to 20 percent of the original amount! Obviously, such persistence implies that Robins can continue to be affected by the pesticide long after its use has been terminated. Eventually, replacement populations may cease to reinhabit the death-trappish area, and in that case Robins (and other afflicted species) will remain locally scarce for a long time to come. The avian vacuum that is thus created may then be filled by species who are not restricted to a diet of worms and insects and so are not as greatly affected by DDT. Quite often these are birds that are not exactly endeared to the human heart—Starlings and Pigeons, for instance, who can subsist on garbage and such things fairly well. Of course, once these new populations become established, they tend to remain; in this way, the ecological effects of DDT can even outlive the chemical itself.

The specific symptoms of DDT poisoning are rather blatant once chemical concentrations reach high levels. Birds lose their sense of balance and cannot fly; tremors set in, some paralysis perhaps, convulsions commence, and then finally death follows within a few hours. In the words of one first-hand observer,

> I found a pair of Robins who were building a nest by Bell Tower. A day later I returned to find the nest completed but the birds on the ground, unable to fly. Both were trembling and the female was near death. The male, despite all this, was trying to sing, but a sadder song was never heard. (Etter, 1963)

Once trembling appears, the individual cannot be saved.

Interestingly enough, and contrary to the implication of the above quote, male Robins appear to be much more susceptible to DDT poisoning than are females. In general, males die sooner, in greater numbers, and at lower DDT levels than do females. This sex difference seems to result from the greater fat reserves that springtime females enjoy. These reserves are capable of storing high concentrations of DDT without bodily harm; thus the fatter females can tolerate more poison than the leaner males.

Solutions to the problem? Development of disease-resistant elms and introduction of biological enemies of the bark beetle (that is, predators, parasites, pathologies) are two possibilities. A third has been the substitution of less potent pesticides for DDT; a chemical called methoxychlor, for example, kills bark beetles, and yet Robins can tolerate it in doses that are thirty times larger than a lethal amount of DDT.

Before we leave this section on pesticidal destruction of Robins, it bears stressing that DDT is not the only villain involved. Other chemicals kill too. In 1972, great numbers of Robins were fatally poisoned in Dade County, Florida, by potato growers who were fighting aphids with a relatively new pesticide, Azodrin. In their enthusiastic application of this chemical cure-all to their crops, the growers inadvertently sprayed a nearby hedge of Christmasberries which, unfortunately, happen to be relished by Robins. So when flocks of hungry Redbreasts subsequently arrived in the area, they eagerly feasted on the berries—their last supper, as it turned out. Within a mere three days, fully ten thousand Robins lay paralyzed or dead. Presumably the potatoes prospered.

So pervasive has been songbird destruction associated with DDT and other pesticidal programs that almost twenty years ago one researcher was moved to warn:

> The current widespread and ever-expanding pesticide program poses the greatest threat that animal

life in North America has ever faced—worse than
deforestation, worse than market hunting and illegal
shooting, worse than drainage, drought or oil pollu-
tion, and possibly worse than all of these decimating
factors combined. . . . If [these programs] are carried
out as now projected, we shall be witnesses to a greater
extermination of animal life than in all the previous
years of man's history on earth, if not since glaciation
profoundly altered the life of the whole Northern
Hemisphere. (Wallace, 1959)

Crop Defense

Except for isolated instances of Robin-killing (for example,
by small boys armed with Christmas-gift air rifles), humans today
do not generally kill Robins intentionally. The bird is, after all, a
friend of good cheer, an ally against the feared and hated insects,
and simply a nice part of Nature to be respected for its own sake.
At least that is usually the case. But it goes without saying that we
humans—who turn viciously upon even ourselves at the slightest
hint of conflicting interests—will turn upon Robins too should
the birds dare to infringe upon our right to every speck of resource
on this planet. We are Earth's supreme creatures and might makes
right.

There are numerous instances from all parts of the continent
where Robins have been slaughtered by the hundreds and thousands because they gathered in some specific farming locality in
search of food. We will return to this topic in the next chapter
when we consider the Robin's feeding habits, but for now let's
look at one specific instance where crop defense motivated Robin-
killing by humans. This example, a recent one, has been graciously provided by blueberry farmers in Canada.

Blueberries, a big crop in New Brunswick, are not a normal
part of Robin foodfare but are certainly acceptable to the fruit-
loving Redbreasts. A blueberry conflict between farmers and

Robins had simmered for years, but finally reached the boiling point (at least publicly) in 1973. The confrontation was allegedly fueled by an "aggressive" pesticide program in the Maritime Provinces, an apparently successful program which greatly diminished bud worms and other insects that Robins had previously depended upon for sustenance. So when their natural foods became unavailable, the birds—strangely reluctant to starve—turned instead to the ripening blueberry crop.

Thus the conflict over blueberries became a desperate question of survival: the farmers depended on the crops for economic livelihood, the Robins for biological existence. A compromise might have seemed in order. But any politician will tell you that conflicting interests between two groups is not in itself a sufficient condition for resolution via compromise; a balance of power is equally vital. And in New Brunswick, at least, the farmers held all the guns.

Blueberry growers had been killing Robins under less pressing circumstances before 1973. The previous year, government permits were routinely granted to eight farmers who together killed an estimated twenty thousand Redbreasts; one man shot seven thousand on his two-hundred-acre farm alone. But in 1973 many more growers applied for permits to exterminate Robins on a truly massive scale, and the sorry sordid spectre of a hundred thousand Robins shotgunned each year in an annual "pest-control" program became imminent. Fortunately, conservation groups in the United States as well as Canada launched a widespread "Robins rather than blueberry pie" campaign to drum up public protest against the killing. And largely in response to the resulting uproar, the Canadian government subsequently denied the permit requests.

The basic problem, of course, had not been solved. The hard-worked crops of blueberry growers were still threatened. We will return to this and other dilemmas of similar sort later, and then consider possible solutions. But of present relevance is speculation on the effects that the Canadian extermination program, had it been endorsed, would have had on the Robin's population.

Obviously, many—no doubt most—American Robins never cross the Canadian border during any part of their life cycle. They hatch, migrate, and breed entirely within the confines of the United States. Consequently the Canadian program—which even within that nation was relatively localized in nature—could not have by itself "endangered" the Robin species as a whole in any direct fashion. The same cannot be said for the particular race of Robins that is largely of Canadian citizenship—the Black-Backed Robin.

Still, one cannot kill fifty to a hundred thousand Robins each year and not produce some depleting effects on the population. Robins are numerous, but their numbers are not infinite. And besides, local killings should not be viewed as merely isolated occurrences but rather as parts of a whole battery of destructive forces exerted upon the Robin's population (the California Condor, remember, was not cast in his present danger by a single folly, but by a host of them). Following New Brunswick's lead, a dozen other local pest-control programs might begin elsewhere, each destroying a hundred thousand Robins annually. Or a rash of ill-conceived pesticide campaigns might suddenly spray their way across North America and poison Robin populations from coast to coast. And in the South, where millions of Robins congregate in dense flocks each winter, millions could die from an unexpected disease, some unstoppable epidemic. Suddenly, Robins could be scarce. Suddenly they could be endangered. And then what would we give to reincarnate those hundred thousand individuals who had died in the blueberry fields of Canada?

In final note, I certainly don't mean to imply that the only reason—or even the most important reason—for not killing Robins is fear for the survival of their species. This cannot be true for *Turdus migratorius* any more than Hiroshima and Nagasaki were lamentable on the grounds that they in themselves constituted threats to *Homo sapiens*. No, much more fundamental values than mere species preservation are involved whenever killing occurs in the absence of absolute necessity.

Robins as Food: An Historical Digression

There is an interesting footnote to this consideration of human-related causes of Robin mortality. Time was, when Robins along with Meadowlarks, Bobolinks, and numerous other songbirds, were classified as "game birds" and were accordingly hunted with vigor. For a number of reasons, such slaughter was largely confined to the southern part of the United States. First, Robins used to (and still do) winter in the South in incalculable flocks, and so could be hunted quite easily, with economy of effort. Then, too, the old South held many poor people who saw no reason why they should remain hungry when they could readily furnish their tables with so abundant a bird. Thirdly and perhaps most importantly, southerners in the past have not held our beloved Robin as close to their hearts as have more northern residents of the United States, and Canadians. Historically, Redbreasts neither sang nor raised their young in the deep South, and these two activities probably mediate as much as anything the northerner's great affection for the species. Instead, Robins were considered by many southern communities as a starling-type of nuisance, especially when their huge flocks damaged cultivated crops.

So Robins were killed without remorse. The following words describe the situation in 1841, as perceived through the eyes of a contemporary:

> In all southern states, the presence of Robins produces a sort of jubilee among gunners, and the havoc made among them with bows and arrows,

blowpipes, guns, and traps of different sorts is wonderful. Every gunner brings them home by bagsful, and markets are supplied with them at a very cheap rate. Several persons may at this season stand round the foot of a tree loaded with berries and shoot for the greater part of a day, so fast do flocks of Robins succeed each other. They are then fat and juicy, and afford excellent eating.

This passage, incidentally, did not arise from the pen of some insignificant peasant. These words of so callous a tone came from none other than John James Audubon, artist of Nature and lover of birds.

You might wonder how anyone could manage to dine on a little ol' Robin in the first place. One Robin, it is true, was hardly worth the trouble of plucking, but then neither is a single fish-egg worth serving. No, Robins were prepared dozen by dozen, and a hundred eggs give you caviar. If at the turn of this century you went shopping in any southern marketplace—or one in Washington, Baltimore, or New York for that matter—you could purchase Robins "by the bunch" at a price ranging from a dime to four bits a dozen. In northern cities where buyers were more likely to hold Robins in some degree of sentimentality, skewered Redbreasts were sold to unknowing consumers under the guise of "rice birds" (Bobolinks, who were also widely eaten, are the true rice birds). Such, then, was the fate of hundreds of thousands of Robins who thus found their way into the markets of America and stomachs of Americans.

How were all these Robins killed? With pitiful ease. Then, as still today, thousands upon thousands of Robins—while wintering in the South—congregated nightly to sleep together within relatively small areas of woods (see Chapter 10, on roosting). Densely packed among branches and sleeping soundly in the dark, the birds made simple prey. At a Robin roost near Fosterville, Tennessee, the carnage transpired like this:

When a party of hunters arrived at the Robin roost at night, one of them with a torch climbed a tree, and when the torch was lighted, the others with poles beat the surrounding trees. Blinded by the light, the suddenly awakened birds flew towards it, and the torch bearer—seizing each one—quickly pulled off its head and dropped the body into a bag hanging from his shoulder. Thus three or four hundred birds were captured by one man in a single night. This tremendous slaughter continued for three or four winters, after which the birds abandoned the roost. (Claxton, as quoted by Forbush, 1929)

Such bloodshed took sufficient tolls on the species that contemporary ornithologists rightly worried that Robins may "soon be classed among our rarer birds." It was not until 1913 that the U.S. Migratory Bird Law attempted to shelter Robins and other songbirds beneath the protective coattails of Uncle Sam. Prior to this, individual states legislated whatever protection, if any, they deemed fit. New York, for example, passed a game law in 1860 that prohibited the shooting or trapping of Robins under penalty of a whopping fifty-cent fine, except during the four months of October through January. In southern states, laws against Robin-killing did not pass until much later (for example, 1912 in Virginia).

Even after the federal law was enacted, it took years of difficult and often sporadic enforcement before the long-practiced customs of southern communities began to change. The following article, published in a 1931 Alabama newspaper, shows what bird crusaders of yesterday (led, incidentally, by the Audubon Society) faced in their tireless campaigns for passage and enforcement of protective legislation:

On Tuesday night a week ago, some Crenshaw citizens met at the Robin roost, or "Hell's Half Acre," to have a bird thrashing like we boys used to have in days gone by. The game warden was made wise and he was also there, but he kept himself under cover until the boys began to thrash the birds. Then he arrested 42 persons for violating the game law, and they have since pled guilty and paid fines of $15.25. They were not there for sport altogether. They were there to get some birds to eat. It is said that some of these people were being fed by the community, and among them was an old Civil War negro, who was told to be down there and they would give him some birds. He was also arrested, so it is said. But the game warden says it was a violation of the Federal Game Law; that we admit, but the law is not based on common sense. At this time the Government is talking about helping our people who are hungry, and these people were after some meat for themselves and families. This law is wrong and there should be an open season on Robins, for they are eating out the pindar fields of this country, so it is said. The majority of our citizens do not endorse the action of the game warden. *(The Dothan Eagle,* 1931— quoted by Pearson, 1931)

Alas, cultural change seems to come ever so slowly when national mandate finds itself confronting local sentiment.

chapter 8

Banquets of Bugs and Berries

As I released the football player from the folds of my mist net, I explained that I was collecting Robins, and that Robins landed on the football field during his scrimmage hours. He made a rude and profane remark. I shrugged, picked up my paraphernalia, then trundled back to a little patch of ground behind the handball courts at San Francisco State College, where I was to spend the next year and a half trying to discover how Robins find worms.

—Frank Heppner, 1967

Robins hunting on a lawn. The sight, so familiar to us all, bespeaks of things unchanging, even eternal, in Nature. The Robin on your grass is not simply a bird looking for food; he is an institution. And he knows it. Look how proudly he carries himself! See the way he flaunts his craft, first standing stone-still erect, then scurrying abruptly, now stopping again. He cocks his head and you know he's found his mark; an instant later, a wiggling worm knows it too.

And worms are not particularly easy to catch. They're difficult to see among stalks of grass, they're quick to retreat into burrows if one's first grab is the merest bit off target, and even when squarely nipped they are tenacious clingers to their tunnels. Yet the Robin, more than any other bird on the continent (probably the world and perhaps the universe), excels at nabbing these miniserpents. He even makes it look easy.

Do I exaggerate the Robin's skill? My gracious no. I once saw a Starling furtively following a Robin across a lawn; whenever the Robin succeeded in pulling up a worm, the Starling made a hopping charge and snatched the snack abandoned by the retreating Redbreast. After swallowing his loot, the black bandit again trailed the Robin and repeated the crime. Numerous other unscrupulous species have been known to similarly exploit the Robin's unparalleled lawn skills, including English Sparrows, Brown Thrashers, and even Sea Gulls. These birds, however, are not thieves because they are lazy; they steal because they are inept. At least when compared to our Robin. Truly, catching worms is not so easy as the redbreasted pro always makes it appear.

We will return to the Robin's worm-hunting habits later, but first let's embark upon a more general survey of his diet. For even a Robin would agree that life is not just a bowlful of annelids.

Natural Diet

The natural food of Robins consists mostly of various wild fruits and numerous small animals. The relative proportions that these two categories contribute to the bird's overall diet changes with both time and place. In fall, for example, when insects become scarce and fruits ripen, vegetal matter may be the Robin's only food; during early summer, on the other hand, the opposite may be largely true. Diet also varies with habitat as Robins living deep in forests will not find as many earthworms as do the Redbreasts who picnic in your backyard. Finally, local concentrations of specific foods may temporarily capture the birds' entire gastronomic attention, as happens during the massive and periodic emergence of seventeen-year locusts. On the whole, however, the Robin's menu consists of approximately 40 percent animal matter and 60 percent vegetal matter.

The animals upon which Robins prey include more than just worms. Fair game are caterpillars, beetles, weevils, grasshoppers, flies, snails, spiders, termites, wasps, and really any larvae the birds can bill. Similarly, hardly a fruit or berry exists that the Robin doesn't like, though he does have his preferences. The varieties are again too numerous to list completely, but a few are cedar berries, dogwood berries, honeysuckle berries, wild cherries, blueberries, blackberries, sumacs, hollies, and mulberries.

Frequently the seeds of these fruits remain viable after passing through the Robin's body, and consequently the bird helps disseminate the plants he patronizes. With cherries and olives, whose pits are too large to pass beyond the stomach, Robins actually disgorge (force back out through the throat) the stones after the fruit's flesh has dissolved. Thus after stuffing himself with cherries, an individual may sit quietly somewhere and then, within a half-hour's time, cough up the stones in a convulsive but satisfying belch. This peculiar process, which results in a pile of clean cherry pits beneath the bird's perch, is comparable to the way in which an owl handles the skulls and bones of mouse victims after swallowing them whole.

Because of the Robin's fondness for fruit, and because fruit ferments rather quickly when the weather is warm, Robins occasionally suffer the role of dupe in one of those amusing little pranks that Mother Nature plays upon her creatures every now and then. For after imbibing their fill of fermented berries, poor unsuspecting Robins show all the signs of inebriation. They flap, flop, flitter, and flutter; they trip, traipse, teeter, and totter; they slip, slide, stumble, and stagger. Sometimes they even pass out. But by the next day they will have recovered sufficient sobriety to fly safely away, birdy hangover and all.

In addition to their basic bug-'n-berry diet, Robins are always ready to dine on more exotic foods should the opportunity arise. Mice, snakes, and fish, for example, are among the rather surprising meals that epicurean Robins have been known to enjoy. Admittedly, the evidence for mouse-munching is scattered and a bit circumstantial: one Robin swallowed a mouse headfirst after the rodent had been killed by a dog; another bird dive-bombed a mouse scurrying across a lawn, killed him in a pecky assault, and then flew away with the corpse; a third Redbreast was seen incubating the headless body of a white-footed mouse in her egg-filled nest (only the eggs hatched, I think); and a fourth Robin, this one an albino, once fought a mole with mutually fatal results.

Robins have several times been known to kill small snakes, including the northern brown snake, the garter snake, and the ribbon snake. With even small serpents, gulping down the reptile is a real problem quite apart from killing him. One Robin staggered around a Florida swamp for twenty minutes with ten inches of half-swallowed snake dangling from his beak, before finally fluttering out of sight. Another drawback of trying to eat these overgrown worms, of course, is that they frequently have an obstinate inclination to defend themselves. Indeed, several Robins have been strangled by sneaky snakes who managed to coil around their would-be consumers.

As for fish, those few Redbreasts who live by lake or sea may habitually visit the shorelines and pretend they are sandpipers, but most fish-eating Robins are only exploiting windfall opportunities. Thus Robins have eaten minnows discarded by fishermen about Wisconsin docks, gobbled up trout fry recently "planted" by wardens in California creeks, and feasted in the shallows of Iowa lakes following ammonia-caused fishkills. Occasionally Robins actually seek out seafood, especially when their traditional terrestrial meals are temporarily unavailable, as occurs following a ground-covering snowstorm or during a lawn-parching drought.

Before we leave the Robin's natural diet, some mention should be made of a bug that is seldom eaten yet often relished by Redbreasts—namely, the ant. Anting, a peculiar behavior performed by many birds, can either involve active insertion of live ants among the feathers, or else passive squatting by which the bird permits ants to crawl within its puffed-out plumage before preening them away. In either case, the accompanying preening movements—which are directed under the wing, along the tail, or around the vent—are often so vigorously violent that the bird staggers or even somersaults for want of balanced restraint.

On one extremely interesting occasion, an anting Robin was repeatedly observed to sweep the litter-covered ground with a twig held in its bill, in apparent efforts to locate the scurrying insects. Such tool-using behavior is rare in the animal kingdom (outside of humans, of course). Wild chimpanzees often poke sticks down termite holes and then, after withdrawing the instrument, lick it clean of clinging insects; sea otters sometimes mash mussel shells against flat stones; solitary wasps typically hammer dirt into burrows with mandible-pinched pebbles; and Egyptian vultures crack thick-shelled ostrich eggs with well-aimed rocks. For various reasons, scientists do not consider all of these tool-using examples as necessarily indicative of unusual intelligence. Even by scientific standards, however, the twig-twirling Robin seems to have portrayed pretty brainy behavior.

Frequently though not always, anting is temporally associated with other body-oriented activities such as sunning and bathing. The exact utility of the strange behavior, however, is still open to question. According to various theories, birds ant in order to: (1) induce sexual or other sensual pleasure; (2) utilize the formic acid or some other substance contained in ants to repel ectoparasites; or (3) soothe, again via ant substances, irritated skin. Since anting occurs most often during August, when the majority of North American birds are molting and hence growing new feathers, the skin-soothing suggestion is favored by many researchers over either the masturbatory or antiparasitic propositions.

Cultivated Crops

The blueberry episode in New Brunswick (Chapter 7) was but one example of Robin depredation of cultivated crops. Besides blueberry fields, Robins have most notably feasted off cherry trees, strawberry patches, olive groves and, to a lesser extent, raspberry gardens and grape vineyards. Figs, pears, prunes, and apples are also occasionally nibbled, but usually in quantities that are quite insignificant and which in any case involve mostly waste fruit passed over as subpar during the previous harvest.

Of the vegetative portion of the Robin's diet, wild fruit accounts for more than ten times as much as cultivated fruit; indeed, less that 5 percent of the species' food in general is human-grown. Many Robins never even have the opportunity to take cultivated food since they live deep in forests or in other areas not inhabited by people. Still, it cannot be disputed that in some cases Robins do real harm to crops. You cannot, after all, have ten thousand fruit-loving Redbreasts sitting in your blueberry field and expect anything less than grand larceny. In the West, where enormous flocks of Robins are sometimes attracted to the olives there, the losses are

> often serious and occasionally disastrous. In some cases it is necessary to employ men with shotguns and keep them constantly firing, in order to save more than 50 percent of the fruit. Some of the birds have as many as six olives in their crops. (Tyler, 1949)

Several points, however, can be made on the Robin's behalf.

First, instances of serious Robin depredation of crops can almost always be traced in origin to regional scarcity of the bird's natural food supply, and these scarcities in turn are often the direct products of human activity. Such was clearly the case in New Brunswick where blueberry banqueting by Redbreasts was precipitated by a pesticide campaign that had obliterated a large part of the bird's normal foodfare. More generally, humans have greatly destroyed the habitats of many wild fruits—through ax, plow, and bulldozer—and this has led to widespread dwindling of that portion of normal Robin sustenance. From whence, then, do we derive the audacity to dispense capital punishment for "crimes" that we ourselves have directly instigated?

Secondly, Robins are without doubt overwhelmingly beneficial to crops because they devour so many insects. Bugs, not birds, are our chief competitors on this planet, particularly where foodstuff is concerned. And do you remember the astronomical numbers we talked of in connection with the potential descendants of a single pair of Robins? Well, those numbers are infinitesimal next to comparable calculations for any insect you care to mention (a single pair of houseflies, for example, has the potential for 191 million trillion descendants *within one year!).* So each time Mother Robin procures a couple of beetles for her nestlings, she is doing far more than saving the farmer's crops from just those two tiny mouths; she is obliterating a potential of billions who—if not negated by Robins and other bug-getters— would soon engulf the world itself, much less a farmer's fields.

Consider this example of the Robin's insect-controlling ability: once in a wooded area where certain insect larvae had become numerous, a flock of about two hundred fifty Robins suddenly appeared and within three weeks had consumed an estimated two hundred thousand of the larvae as well as twenty-one thousand beetles and sixty-six thousand members of a large insect order called Hemiptera; together, these dispatched bugs accounted for approximately 80 percent of the entire invertebrate population living within the local forest litter. Similarly impressive insect ingestion has often been spectacularly instrumental in crop salvation; Robins have been properly credited with saving southern cotton crops from weevil wreckage, Massachusetts cranberry bogs from white grub demolition, Texan grain from armyworm annihilation, and Ohio hayfields from Marchfly mastication.

Even in the absence of such obvious heroism, however, Robins are always quietly but effectively going about their insect-checking work, to the most direct benefit of the farmer. Yet despite this good reason for accepting Robins as allies, some people persist in viewing them as foes. Thus the following words, now so old, could still apply today:

> I have known instances where a Robin who had saved from ten to fifteen bushels of apples that were worth a dollar per bushel, by clearing the trees from canker-worms in the Spring, was shot when he simply pecked one of the apples that he had saved for the ungrateful fruit-grower. (Merriam, 1898)

Under conditions of moderation, then, it would seem that Robins rightfully deserve at least some portion of the crops they save, as justly earned retribution. But how can moderation be preserved? Of the several methods available—all of which, by the way, are fairly effective—perhaps the easiest and most commonly used has been the shotgun approach. Despite its popularity, however, this method is thricely flawed since it destroys a largely beneficial bird, defiles the reverence that all Nature warrants, and demeans the human spirit. Better alternatives exist.

In the case of blueberries, for example, nets can shield the fruit from birds; while obviously not in use in New Brunswick, such nets are effectively employed as a matter of course by many blueberry growers in the United States. In similar fashion, cherry trees can be screened from avian snacking. Considerable expense, it is true, is involved with such nets and screens, but governmental subsidy can reasonably be expected for such purposes. Preservation of wildlife, after all, is not a responsibility that should be borne alone by farmers or any other single segment of society, but by us all.

A really nice solution to the problem involves the strategic planting of attractive wildfruit near cultivated crops. Mulberry bushes are excellent for this purpose as they are vigorous in growth, bountiful in berries, timely in ripening, and absolutely adored by Robins. Thus if a few mulberry bushes stand near orchard or field, Robins will be only too happy to dine on those berries and leave the cherries and blueberries to the farmer. The birds' policing of insects, meanwhile, will still continue unabated.

In summary, then, we might characterize the Robin's relationship with cultivated crops as overridingly beneficial, by virtue of the species' continuous destruction of crop-consuming insects. And on those occasions where Robins would indeed be significantly harmful to the farmer's fruits—occasions that are frequently inspired by human actions—the birds can be either blocked or enticed away from the crops in lieu of being shot.

The Lawn Patrol

Just before a Robin plunges at a worm, he cocks his head in the direction of his prey. This cocking movement has given many people, including early ornithologists, the natural impression that the bird is listening intently for faint sounds of earthworms moving within their burrows. Since most avian predators locate their food by sight rather than sound, the redbreasted hunter seemed in this respect to be something of an oddball. It remained until only recently that scientists determined conclusively how Robins actually find worms.

Possible cues that Robins might employ in their hunting include vibrations (arising from the worm's movements), odors, sounds, and sights. Vibrations, however, were promptly ruled out by the observation that the heavy rumblings of nearby trucks and streetcars did not interfere with a Redbreast's lawn success. Worm odors also seemed unimportant since Robins—like most birds—apparently have rather atrocious sniffers; in one of several tests, foul tidbits were presented to a captive Robin who

> nonchalantly ate foods smelling like rotten eggs, decaying meats, rancid butter, and the absolutely worst of all bad smells, mercaptoacetic acid, which has been described as a cross between sewer gas, rotten cabbage, a skunk, and a stinkbug. (Heppner, 1967)

The potential role of hearing was then eliminated by the researchers when artificial background noise—noise loud enough to mask any possible sounds made by earthworms—did not stop Robins from cocking their heads and finding their worms. Finally, vision was pinpointed as the crucial sense when dead worms that had been preserved in alcohol (and hence were vibrationless, odorless, and soundless) were easily found and readily gobbled by unfinicky Redbreasts. In conclusion, then, Robins most assuredly see, and not feel, smell, or hear, the worm who drills its subterranean home beneath your lawn.

So why does the Robin so characteristically cock his head? Simple: his eyes, being on the side of his head, make it difficult to see close-range objects that are directly in front of him; he sees them better if they are on his flank. So by turning and cocking his head, he is simply centering the visual field of one eye upon the target before launching his pouncing attack. Worms, incidentally, being ever prepared for hasty retreat, frequently catnap with only the tips of their bodies protruding from their tunnels. It is this tip o' worm that Robins must discover, focus upon, and grab with unerring accuracy.

Besides head-cocking, another striking characteristic of the Robin's hunting habits is the zig-zag nature of his movements. First he's running toward you, but then after a pause he's off in an entirely different direction, and so on *ad infinitum*. Should other Robins be simultaneously patrolling the same field, as indeed they often are, the resulting scene is that of a leaderless flock whose members can't decide which way to proceed as they run hither and thither in apparent confusion. Actually, two separate factors largely determine the zany nature of these foraging movements.

The zig-zag business, first of all, is largely the product of sheer laziness. Since their eyes are virtually immovable within their respective sockets, Robins must turn their whole heads to look in a given direction. Rather than rotate their heads a full quarter-turn—as would be necessary to look straight ahead—they just turn a little bit and, should the view be at all promising, promptly scamper off thataway. Then when they subsequently repeat the process, they may focus with the other eye and so embark upon an entirely different course.

A second factor affecting the Robin's lawn navigation involves the specific body orientations of nearby companions. Since the red breast seems to be an aggression-eliciting sight for the species, two birds who face each other head-on are likely to skirmish. Being more intent upon food than battle, Robins try to avoid such confrontations during group feeding and so tend to not orient breast to breast with each other. This avoidance of breasting thus imposes a restriction upon the direction of a Robin's movements; having spied worm signs in the distance, an individual will head off in that direction only if doing so will not bring him face to face with a conspecific. Of course, this antipathy toward breasting on community feeding grounds is not absolute. Robins do occasionally face each other and then fight, especially during early spring when hostility runs high. For the most part, however, such orientations are less frequent than they would otherwise be.

Given the mutual antagonism that is at least potentially present during communal hunting, why do Robins bother to gather on the same field in the first place? Why don't they just avoid each other entirely and secure food outside of community cafeterias? True, a flock of feeding Robins has many watchful eyes to preclude surprise attacks by predators; Robins do have excellent group-warning signals, particularly in the form of loud calls that quickly send a foraging flock flapping for foliage. But Robins periodically feed singly throughout the day (communal feeding occurs primarily during the early morning) and still manage to survive, so group protection would not seem to be the selective advantage that encourages flockly hunting.

In many birds, like soaring Sea Gulls, group feeding accrues real benefits since any discovery by one individual is quickly shared by all. But Robins certainly do not share worms with each other, and so this factor is not the answer either. This perplexing problem of Robin sociability during a time when their spirits are generally spleenful will emerge again when we consider the roosting habits of Redbreasts (Chapter 10). And unfortunately, a satisfactory resolution will be as evasive in that context as it is in the present one.

Before we close this chapter, sensitivity suggests that we embark upon an excursion of empathy and say a word about the worm. In their largely underground world, worms continuously work for environmental good and seem to cause no one any harm in the process. The earthworm, indeed, may be the single most important animal living in the soil. Tirelessly tilling the tough terrain, *Lumbricus terrestris* enriches the earth with excretions and aerates the land with burrows. Equally important, the earthworm is prey for a veritable menagerie of life ranging from microorganisms and insects through all the vertebrate families, including fish (ask any fisherman), amphibians (frogs and toads), reptiles (snakes and turtles), birds (an example escapes me), and a multiplicity of mammals (moles, shrews, skunks, and armadillos, to name a few). Through enormity of number—Charles Darwin once estimated some sixty-four thousand earthworms residing per acre—the annelid army brings as much as two inches of earth to the surface every ten years, a process invaluable to the health of the soil.

In addition to their ecological importance, earthworms have been major teachers in the science of anatomy, as any zoology student who's ever held a scalpel will surely attest. Earthworms, furthermore, are intelligent. Well, at least they are not so dumb as their humble appearance would suggest. Worms seem able to learn, for example, which way to turn in a maze when a reward of moisture awaits them in the goalbox.

The point of all this is that everytime we see a Robin succeed in upping and downing a worm, we should realize that the episode represents not only the admirable execution of rare avian skill, but also the regrettable termination of one very fine animal. And the Robin would be the first to tell you so.

chapter 9

Rockin' Robin

Nothing more startling in a bird way ever happened to me than during a drill by the Hawaiian police (June 17, 1936), when one of their number came out and did a whistling stunt. There was an audience of some twenty-five thousand that witnessed the show in the Multnomah Stadium; and soon after the man began to whistle, about 11 P.M., a Robin came down out of the darkness onto the field within a few feet of the whistler (the field was lighted by high-powered flood-lights), and sang as long as the whistling continued. Many of us thought it was a prearranged stunt, but as soon as the whistling was over, the Robin flew away into the darkness.

—Harold S. Gilbert, as
quoted by Tyler, 1949

No two snowflakes, we're told, are exactly alike; each has sufficient individuality to make it a unique entity. Similarly, no two Robins sing their morning carol in exactly the same way. Each Redbreast strings phrases and accents notes just a little bit differently than any of his neighbors. There are, to be sure, underlying qualities that characterize the musical talents of the species as a whole. But when meticulously analyzed as some scientists have done, each Robin's song turns out to be, like the delicate snowflake, a unique creation unduplicated in our universe. And there is something wonderful in that.

In addition to their basic carol, Robins boast an impressive variety of other vocalizations. Their repertoire is so extensive, in fact, that only those listeners who are most familiar with the species can consistently recognize each song and call. Nevertheless, we can try to summarize at least the highlights of Robin vocabulary. First, though, let's look specifically at the Robin's renowned morning carol, that cheerful melody which bursts upon one's senses with as much invigorating inspiration as the crimson rays of the rising sun.

Cheer-up, Cheerily

The Robin's bread-'n-butter song is basically a string of two- and three-note phrases that continue, with variation, for an indefinite period of time. Translated into human tongue, the sound is most frequently represented as something akin to "cheer-up, cheerily; cheer-up, cheer-up, cheerily." But different listeners prefer different syllabifications. Thus did Dr. Leroy Titus Weeks in 1923 offer the world his now-infamous rendition of the Robin's song:

Pillywink, pollywog, poodle, poodle,
Pollywog, poodle, pillywink, pillywink,
Poodle, poodle, pillywink, pollywog,
Poodle, poodle.

Nothing so consistently brings a smile to my face—except, perhaps, hearing the Robin's morning carol—as does reading Dr. Weeks' fantastic verbiage.

Generally speaking, only male Robins sing, although females do give various short calls that warn of predators and the like. This male monopoly of melody is not too surprising given that the primary utilities of Robin song are territorial defense (which falls mainly within the male's realm of responsibility) and sexual advertisement (if *both* sexes sang to attract mates, much awkward confusion could mark the meeting of, say, two females on the prowl). Often the male has a favorite rooftop or perch within his territory where he likes to sing. Like many songbirds, Robins appear to prefer a certain "minimum height" for a song perch, and they are reluctant to sing at heights lower than this minimum. These heights vary from species to species, and for the Robin it is about a dozen feet—relatively high as minimum singing heights go. This preference is not rigid, however, and Robins will occasionally deliver a chorus while foraging on a lawn. A bar or two may also be uttered on the wing.

Admittedly, the Robin is not the greatest of bird singers either in terms of tonal quality (compared to, for instance, a Hermit or Wood Thrush) or in terms of improvisation (compared to a Mockingbird). Nevertheless, Rockin' Robin brandishes an above-average tune. And what he lacks in fine artistry is more than compensated for by his enthusiasm, which in itself is enough to stir an appreciative wiggle from any human ear. Like an eagerly auditioning trumpeter, the Robin throws back his head, blasts out his song, and utterly drowns out competing minstrels of other species. We might resent the way he confidently dominates the morning air were his zesty music not so pleasing to hear.

Do Robins sing all year round, or are there months in which they are silent? The general answer is that Robins sing primarily during their breeding season and are pretty songless the rest of the time. Robins are almost completely silent during spring migration, for example, unlike the majority of American birds who typically arrive at their breeding grounds with a song in their hearts and a tune on their beaks. Within a few days to a week after arriving in the North, however, our Robin is crooning up and down his territorial boundaries as he determinedly warns other males to keep away while simultaneously extending warm invitations to any fair maiden within earshot.

Once begun in April, such singing continues until the end of summer. Then, during August, the music becomes increasingly thin as more and more individuals drop out of the Robin choir; by September, nearly all the males are generally silent except for an occasional outburst or two now and again. A slight resurgence may occur around October, but for the most part the Robin carol is kaput until the following spring. Except for various call notes, Robins are more or less silent during their winter stay in the South.

It is impossible, of course, to pinpoint precise dates of song initiation and cessation from year to year, or even for the species as a whole during a given year. The initiation of song will vary by a matter of weeks, both with the latitude of a given locality (since migrants arrive much later at locations as far north as Canada compared to locations in the Mid-Atlantic states), and with the particular year (since migration proceeds more quickly during mild springs that during harsh ones). And of course there are always large individual differences among Robins, so that even during a given year at a given location, one individual may start (or stop) singing long before another individual does. Nevertheless, the above-noted pattern of song is still generally true for the Robin population as a whole.

We might now ask whether—during the singing season—Robins warble continuously throughout the day. Generally, they do not. To be sure, in early April when territories are in flux and mates are being won, a male may sing almost nonstop from dawn till dusk. But soon his cantillations are largely restricted to early morning and evening hours, being perhaps a bit more subdued in the evening. Robins may, however, sing at any time of day if the sky is cloudy. Why should gloomy clouds spur an otherwise silent

Robin into gleeful vocal expression? The answer lies within the fact that, like many other songbirds, the Robin's singing is strongly regulated by the intensity of the light around him.

Robins typically begin their morning carol in dim light (around .02 foot-candles), which explains why they are among the earliest of our singers; most other species wait until the rising sun makes the world hundreds of times brighter before whistling their first note. Naturally, atmospheric conditions affect the Robin's daily starting time, which is earlier on crisp mornings resplendent with moonbeams and later on overcast mornings veiled with clouds. The dimming light at dusk again stimulates the Robin to sing, as do midday clouds or even eclipses.

Once when I was visiting Chicago I heard a Robin sing outside my bedroom window at ungodly hours of the night (between 1:00 A.M. and 3:00 A.M.). The particular neighborhood I was in, however, just happened to be unusually well-illuminated at night by powerful crime-preventing street lamps. Apparently these beacons of safety were sufficiently strong to maintain a light intensity above the caroling threshold of some bleary-eyed but still cheery Robin.

A less surprising result of this light intensity factor is that Robins sing earlier in the morning at higher latitudes than at lower ones, since daylight arrives sooner at the higher. While my Chicago crooner was unusual at his 42°N latitude, one-in-the-morning ballads are not rare at 60°N latitude (say in northern Quebec). And in keeping with our altitude-equals-latitude principle (described in Chapter 2), we would expect mountain-dwelling Redbreasts to receive the sun's first rays sooner, and so begin their morning carol earlier, than valley-living birds.

If light intensity modifies the timing of the Robin's daybreak chorus along the dimensions of latitude and altitude, so too it must in way of longitude. Since morning arrives in the East before the West, Boston Robins sing sooner than Seattle Robins.

Such an obvious point would not be worth mentioning were it not for the charmingly picturesque allusion to the matter that has been made in the past.

"On every vernal morning," a poetic ornithologist once remarked, "a wave of Robin song rises on the Atlantic coast to hail the coming day, and so, preceding the rising sun, rolls across the land until at last it breaks and dies away upon the distant shores of the Pacific Ocean." Oh, if only we humans could cast off the blindfold of spatial limitation and actually perceive this daily wave! We surely then would witness one of the great dramatic events of Nature. Still, whether we perceive it or not, this grand Robin opera continues to salute each summer dawn as it has faithfully done since time immemorial.

Various Other Vocalizations

Now let's look at some other aspects of Robin parlance. We humans may not always be able to interpret these vocalizations with complete appropriateness. No doubt the Robins themselves, however, converse in the birdy lingo rather fluently.

The Robin's *courtship song* is sung almost exclusively during April, when mister is wooing missus. This moving melody is similar to the carol except that it is much softer. With closed bill, the male whispers sweet nothings to his newly chosen bride who, most likely, is but a yard or two away.

Resembling the courtship song is the *rain song*, which also is a soft under-the-breath sort of tune. Given during the darkness that precedes a summer storm, this rain song is apparently only a subdued version of the morning carol sung in response to the decreased intensity of light that foreboding clouds bring. From a somewhat less scientific perspective, the whistling Robins appear to be stirred to merriment by the pleasing proposition of wiggling worms driven to surface by the upcoming downpour.

The *warning call* is a high-pitched note that Robins sound at the sight of a flying predator, such as a hawk. Interestingly, military planes flying in formation have also been known to evoke these warning calls from wary Robins. This do-it-yourself air-raid siren is usually accompanied by "freezing" (remaining motionless) on the part of the Redbreast who initiates it, and the sound itself in turn elicits freezing from other Robins who hear it. Even members of other species—including, remarkably, domestic chickens—will freeze when the Robin alert is given. Typically, freezing lasts as long as the call continues, which may mean anywhere from ten seconds to ten minutes. Should a Robin be caught out in the open when the warning call is sounded—if, for example, he is feeding on a shelterless lawn—he will probably first fly up into the nearest bush or tree before becoming statuesque.

In one interesting report, a month-old human-reared Robin suddenly stopped preening and froze when he heard the warning call of Robins outside his room, even though curtains shielded all the windows so that he could not possibly have seen the predator outside. This same fledgling had himself given the warning call when, at the mere age of eighteen days, he had detected a Cooper's Hawk flying by the window. With little doubt, then, the warning call is largely an instinctive response to a flying predator since this human-reared orphan could not have learned how to give the call, or how to respond to it, from either his natural parents or any other adult Robins.

This anecdote, incidentally, brings up the more general question of how Robins develop their own brand of song. In one experiment that studied the morning carol, some Robins were separately raised from hatch in complete isolation from all other Robins, so that the birds never heard any conspecifics sing. These isolated individuals subsequently developed a carol that was recognizably characteristic of a Robin, but was definitely abnormal in that the phraseology was untypically simple. In other words, a baby Robin must be able to hear other Robins sing before it will develop a "normal" carol of its own.

In this same study, a second group of Robins were experimentally deafened right after they hatched so that they could not even hear themselves sing. These deaf Redbreasts developed an extremely abnormal song—barely more than a series of disconnected notes and scarcely recognizable as sounds made by a Robin. It would appear, then, that for normal development of at least the carol, a baby Robin needs to hear other Robins sing, but that hearing one's own self is better than nothing. Other vocalizations such as the warning call may, as noted above, be more instinctive in nature.

Well, let us continue our survey of Robin vocabulary. When Robin parents see a cat or perhaps a squirrel near their nest, they begin a *cat call* which has been described as a "wailing cry" expressing "both fear and sorrow." This woeful wail may eventually evolve into a screaming shriek as an audacious attack is launched, and the resulting ruckus will quickly rally other raucous Redbreasts to the skirmish site. Diving and screeching and occasionally delivering actual blows against the hated intruder, the winged troops are usually able to drive the enemy away.

Still another Robin antagonist who typically receives an abrasively vocal greeting is the owl. Habitually, owls rest during the day, and toward this end they try to find a quiet secluded patch of foliage for napping. Should a Robin happen to discover a snoozing owl, however, fireworks start to fly. A *mobbing call* is given and within minutes, numerous Robins and assorted other songbirds are screaming, diving, and in general harassing the bewildered predator until he finally departs in pursuit of more peaceful surroundings.

Then there is the Robin's *food call* which is given by fledglings who, hiding in bushes, thereby make their presence and hunger known to their parents (usually their father). This call is a bit risky, of course, since through it a cat or dog may locate the youngster before his parents do. So parentally irresistible is the drawing power of this call that neighboring Robins who have eggs, nestlings, or even fledglings of their own may nonetheless be seduced into bringing tasty morsels to a plaintive bush-baby who belongs to someone else. And, as with the mobbing call, birds of other species may also respond to a young Robin's food call. Once a male Cardinal, whose own nestlings had perished in a storm, fed nearby Robin fledglings so faithfully that they soon followed him closely as he foraged about the lawn.

In summary, the Robin has a host of songs and calls, each one of which reflects a characteristic mood or crisis. Technically speaking, we must concede that our Robin is not a truly master musician, at least compared to some of the other more talented thrushes. Yet in the final analysis, we judge bird song not by its musical quality nor even by its creativeness, but by its effect on the human spirit. And when measured by *this* standard, the song of Robins—whether sweet carols telling of springtime promise, courtship whispers inviting communions of love, or war cries whooped in defense of young—is surely among Nature's most moving sounds.

chapter 10

Roostville, North America: A Robin Metropolis

> At sunset the sky is black with Robins coming in to roost, and at daybreak when they are leaving the sound is like a train passing over a long trestle.
>
> —Observer at Alabama
> Robin roost, 1931

Each of us, probably, hides something about ourselves—something secret, something dark, something perhaps even sinister. I know I do. And no matter how openly we may relate to other people, we always have within us one or two very personal facts that would startle our best friend or spouse were they to discover them. It should come as no surprise, then, that the Robin—that trusting, sincere, straightforward-appearing fellow —should keep his own little secrets as well, certain habits that are little known and even less understood. But for me, nothing about the Robin's behavior remains as baffling or as intriguing as his habit of roosting.

By "roosting," I refer to the Robin's practice of flocking in one place to spend the night. Although the mammoth winter roosts that Robins form in the South had been known to ornithologists for a long time, the birds' summer roosts remained unreported until much later—near the turn of this century, which is remarkably recent considering how well-known a bird the Robin is. Even today the fact that Robins roost in flocks each night is news to most laymen, while many fundamental questions about the phenomenon have yet to be adequately answered even by scientists.

Who Roost?

As soon as they reach their breeding grounds in spring—even before the females arrive—male Robins begin congregating in roosts at night. Already a perplexing mystery is posed: How can a bird who spends all day vigorously defending his territory against redbreasted conspecifics suddenly surrender his pugnacious spirit and actively seek the companionship of his fellows? What magic is this that turns a lustful daytime gladiator into an affable fraternity brother at night? Whatever the potion, its Jekyll and Hyde effects are spectacular!

Though females too spend evenings at the roost when they first arrive after migration, they do not do so throughout most of the summer. Alas, for the most part, while the males hold their nightly stag gatherings, the females are stuck home incubating their eggs and brooding their young. Even when the first brood has finally fledged and become airborne, Pop Robin takes his speckled youngsters to the roost while Mom begins the egg-laying and incubating chores that the season's second brood necessitates. It is only after this second batch of young is fledged that the females—finally freed from family functions—fly roostward with the males as part of their daily routine.

All of this means that roosts which begin with mere dozens of males in the spring grow dramatically in size as first broods, second broods, and finally females join the Robin ranks each evening. By mid-September, hundreds and even thousands of Robins flock together as if to celebrate the end of another successful season of species proliferation. These noisy nocturnal gatherings continue until fall migration commences, and then the once-bustling roost becomes empty and abandoned until the following spring.

In addition to increases from the local population, however, contributions to the roost's numbers also occur in early autumn when premature migrants—originally from other breeding locations but now passing through the area—follow local residents to their bedchambers. For a specific example, let's drift back and listen to one of the two pioneer reports on Robin roosts:

> Some of the Robins appeared to be ignorant of the precise whereabouts of the roost. . . . I took special note of one fellow who came from the South at a great altitude and went directly over the wood. When he was well past it he suddenly pulled himself up, as if fancying he had caught a signal. After a moment of hesitation he proceeded on his northerly course, but had not gone far before he met half a dozen birds flying south. Perhaps he asked them the way. At all events, he wheeled about and joined them, and in half a minute was safe in port. Apparently, he had heard of the roost (how and where?), but had not before visited it. (Torrey, 1890)

Incidentally, at almost precisely the time Bradford Torrey made public his rather startling, if anthropomorphic, observations on summer Robin roosts, a similar revelation was being effected by fellow New Englander William Brewster. This apparently constituted a case of that type of simultaneous but independent discovery—reminiscent of the Wallace-Darwin breakthrough concerning evolution—which comprises a most interesting sidelight in the history of science.

In addition to their summer roosts, Robins, as mentioned earlier, also form roosts during their winter stay in the South. These roosts, drawing on Robins who have migrated from all parts of the continent, are sometimes immense beyond accurate description. Roosts covering a hundred acres have held what conservative observers estimate to be upwards of fifty thousand birds. One forty-acre tract of Alabama swampland, used as a roosting site during the late 1920s, attracted Robins in "almost inconceivable numbers," estimated at fully a million Redbreasts by one perhaps exaggerating observer.

Where Roost?

Almost any area of dense vegetation, with many young saplings and plenty of thick (and preferably berry-laden) shrubbery, will serve as a roosting site for Robins. Often the location will be relatively remote from human habitation; frequently it has a field or lawn nearby where pre-bedtime snacks can be gotten, as well as a stream or brook for drinks and baths. Secluded woods within golf courses or cemeteries, as well as relatively inaccessible swamps, appear to be especially attractive roosting spots.

Under certain circumstances, though, Robins will even roost in open fields, among grasses and clover less than six inches high. Such roofless roosting seems to involve migrating individuals who were unceremoniously forced down by suddenly bad weather—high winds, rain, snow. Any port in a storm, you know. But these emergency bivouacs are rarities; Robins much more typically rest at long-established encampments that are well hidden within luxuriant foliage.

Yet the exact manner by which Robins settle upon one particular place to locate their roost is a real mystery. Other sites near a given roost may actually afford better protection or offer more abundant food than the roost itself. And although Robins— if unduly persecuted at their roost by man or beast—will move to another location, they sometimes suddenly abandon roosts that have been faithfully used for a decade or more, without any discernible reason whatsoever. No doubt it is the mature and experienced birds who guide the general Robin population to a given roost (as, for example, when fathers lead their young). But how new roosts are initially established and why old ones are eventually abandoned remains a puzzle.

Methods of Approach

Except for juveniles who follow their fathers, Robins heading roostward typically travel in loose flocks, reminding one of last-minute Christmas shoppers who, though doing the same thing together, nevertheless do it with a distinct air of mutual independence. The exact manner of approach to the roosting area varies from roost to roost and even from night to night.

Sometimes Robins will fly close to the tree-tops, stopping here and there along the way as if the distance were too great for them to traverse at once (which of course it is not). At other times the birds may come in a continuous flight at great heights—so great that their bodies are difficult to see against the dimming sky; then, when finally above the roost, they fold in their wings and drop into the foliage like a hailstorm of wounded ducks. At still other times, Robins skim along the ground as they approach the roost, weaving to and fro among tree-trunks and bushes. What determines these different flight patterns is unclear, although important factors probably include weather (flight altitude may be lowered during rough, windy weather) and the total distance from nest-to-roost (Robins traveling five miles to the roost each night may fly sky-high while those coming from a mile or less may hopscotch along the tree-tops).

At a cemetery roost I visited in Pennsylvania, scattered groups of Robins appeared to approach the general vicinity of the roost by flying at tree-top heights with periodic rest-stops. Most arrived with a good hour of daylight remaining, and during that time they fed in typical Robin fashion on the lawns of nearby homes as well as on the neatly groomed grass of the cemetery itself. As they foraged they gradually hopped their way toward the roost, which sat at the bottom of a long sloping hill gravely landmarked with tombstones. By the time the light was quite dim, most Robins were within three hundred yards of the roost, and the flock covered this final stretch of ground by nearly simultaneous flight.

Like leaves hurled by a strong autumn wind, dozen upon dozen of auburn Robins skimmed over the ground just above the tips of vertical gravemarkers. More than once as I sat perfectly still on the cemetery lawn, I felt sure my head would abruptly meet the beak of some careless individual who—caught up in the excitement of the flight—might fail to swerve aside in time. But fortunately, my head (which cannot afford any leaks) remained unpunctured by the skillful flyers.

Robins, incidentally, do not always roost by themselves but instead are often joined by one or more other species of bird. Grackles, Cowbirds, Swallows, Cow Buntings, Thrashers, Blackbirds, Cedarbirds, and Orioles are just a few of the congenial species who sometimes share sleeping accommodations with Robins. Usually the different species intermingle among the branches, but at one roost I noticed that numerous Crows slept in strict segregation a hundred or so yards from the Robins. Multi-species roosts are interesting to visit because they usually provide contrasting examples of roost-arrival, with some species (for example, Starlings) flying in tight flock formation while others—like our Robin—approach in small loose groups or even singly.

Survival Value

Why, we may now ask, do Robins roost together instead of simply spending the night in their own individual territories? Perhaps more pointedly, why should the males each evening desert not only their territories but their mates as well? It's difficult to say. Despite the fact that Robins usually select heavily vegetated areas for their roosts, they nonetheless are no safer there than they would be at their nest sites. In fact, just the opposite may be true. Scattered out in their respective territories, Robins could never suffer concentrated predation at night; but gathered together in densely populated roosts they become much more vulnerable—even a single predator can wreak considerable havoc among them. Indeed, bobcats and other nocturnal predators are especially attracted to these roosting areas, where they can feast to heart's content among the soundly snoring sleepers.

One benefit of roosting, however, might be the preparation it affords young Robins for the mammoth undertaking of fall migration. Not only can the daily flights help strengthen the developing wing muscles of young birds, but through these minitrips youngsters can also develop the habit of following their parents, and at the same time gain experience in navigating over at least short distances. These factors may prove important preliminaries to the impending migratory voyage. Roosting and migratory behavior, by the way, are interestingly similar, for in both cases Robins cast aside their territorial imperative and become flockers, showing a characteristic restlessness in the meanwhile. And both roosting and migration constitute major rhythms—daily and yearly, respectively—in the ebb and flow of Robin existence.

Roosting Sensations

Strange sounds and sights await an observer at a Robin roost. First, there is the flapping of winged multitudes as they enter the roost, each bird silhouetted for a fleeting instant against the dimly lit sky. The predawn exodus the next morning is even more impressive since the birds leave the roost more simultaneously than they entered it. At some of the larger winter roosts in the

South, where thousands of Robins are in the air at the same time, the resulting stimulation can awe one's perception (as suggested by the quote at the beginning of this chapter). At a three-hundred-acre South Carolinian roost whose population was estimated at fifty thousand Robins, one local resident went so far as to claim that when birds flew in, his head could feel wind generated by their wings! This man apparently was either short on hair or tall on tales.

Then there is the flutter of wings within the leafy roost as newly arrived birds attempt to secure an unoccupied twig among overpopulated branches. Usually this constant rustle combines with general bird-talk which, because of the innumerable conversationists involved, amounts to a rocky surf roar. Indeed, a lone observer standing among thousands of fluttering and squabbling Robins in the dense vegetation of a darkened roost can, with just a little imagination, experience the same sort of subtle fear that overtakes one amid screeching parrots and wailing monkeys in the Amazon's deepest jungle.

Even after night passes and all the birds have departed for their respective territories, a Robin roost is still worth a sightseeing trip or two. Now quiet and deserted, it is a place to linger and reflect upon the booming population it hosted only hours before, and which it will once again hold a few hours hence. Like an historic Nevada silver-mining town, the daytime Robin roost seems a rather ghostly site. Were teeming hordes really there so short a while ago? Indeed, in the blunt reality of the shining sun you might even deny the events of the preceding night were it not for the Robin snow all around you.

Henry David Thoreau used the term "Robin snow" to refer to a springtime storm that fell after Robins had arrived from the South, but for me the term has quite another meaning: the white droppings of thousands of Robins which accumulate night after night on the ground beneath the birds' perches like just so much winter precipitation. This snow will be the only daytime testimony bearing indisputable witness of the nightly visitations of *Turdus migratorius* to the silent, empty woods where you now stand.

There are, then, many mysteries surrounding the Robin's secretive habit of roosting. Questions abound concerning the bird's sudden congeniality, the nature of his approach flight, his choosing of particular sites and his abandonment of others, and the exact biological adaptiveness of the roosting habit itself—all these questions are still answered by scientific speculation rather than documented fact. But to at least get a proper perspective on how roosting fits into the Robin's daily routine, we might quickly summarize a Robin's activities on a typical midsummer day.

Upon awakening an hour or so before dawn when the sky still sparkles with stars, Father Robin leaves the roost and returns to his mate, who has slumbered on her nest. He then spends the day singing, defending territory, and helping to feed and protect any nestlings or fledglings that he and his mate may have. As twilight approaches, our avian commuter sings a final tune from his favorite perch, bids goodnight to his "lady," and takes off for Roostville, perhaps with other males from his neighborhood and certainly with his juvenile young tagging dependently behind.

chapter 11

Change of Life

Most of us know the American Robin only in its breeding season—that quarter or third of the year when it compromises with its natural wildness and, like city squirrels and pigeons, accepts a measure of domesticity, nesting against our houses and getting its living from our lawns and gardens. It shows its adaptiveness in this, because as soon as it is released from family responsibilities it returns to the kind of woodland life it must have led before man came to America. In late summer, fall, and winter the Robins live in loose flocks within the borders of woods and fly from a person in alarm before he has got close enough to discover their presence. It is hard to understand such wild mistrust of man among birds that have recently sought the shelter of his habitation for their nesting.
                                    —Louis J. Halle, Jr., 1965

One fundamental principle of Robinology is that the birds never seem to be friendly toward both humans and other Redbreasts at the same time. While at their nighttime summer roosts, for example, Robins are relatively affable toward each other and yet nervously suspicious of people. Such sentiments, however, are in sharp contrast with their daytime affections throughout the breeding season, for the then-territorial Robins are quite hostile toward their fellows but show remarkable tolerance—sometimes downright chumminess—toward humans. Indeed, backyard Redbreasts can sometimes be coaxed into accepting tidbits from the hand, and in one case, a Robin habitually followed a man about the neighborhood—without any food inducement whatsoever—so long as the gentleman "talked to it in a low, confidential tone" (Forbush, 1929).

As noted by Halle, however, this friendliness toward people dies with autumn's fading leaves. By September, Robins have not only begun flocking in apparent enjoyment of each other's company, but are also beginning to flee from humans with all the timidity of skittish mountain sheep. It is at this season that a person can walk quietly into a wooded area which hides hundreds of Robins, only to "hear a rustling in the foliage, a soft 'whut-whut,' and all vanish unseen" (Bent, 1949). Fall, then, marks a temperamental change of life for the Robin, a time when humans become feared rather than trusted, a time when fellow Redbreasts become comrades rather than adversaries.

The Robin's diet reflects a second change that ensues with the coming of autumn. All spring and most of summer, the birds feast upon the wealth of invertebrate life that exuberates everywhere. By fall, however, worms have retired far underground and most insects have either died or are hibernating in cloistered retreat. Forced to find other foodfare, Robins turn to the abundant wild berries that now burst forth in ripened glory. Thus, at summer's end, Robins shift from an animal menu to a vegetative one.

Yet another change is that of apparel, for fall is also a time for molting. To the year's youngsters, molting means a loss of speckled vests and the donning of adult garb; for the adults themselves, molting means a change from bright breeding outfits to more subdued attire (to duller breasts). During the short period necessary for these transformations, Robins retire to sheltered, wooded areas where they can doze, preen, and eat in sluggish, solitary silence. Their sociable spirits reappear with their new suits, however, and soon the birds return to their flocks. The rest of autumn is then spent wandering from one berry patch to another as the Redbreasts build up their fat reserves in anticipation of the impending journey south. Thus fall marks still another change of life for the Robin, namely, the shift from sedentary breeding existence to more nomadic ways. Let us now turn to the highlight of this nomadism—the fall migration.

Fall Migration

Lacking the promissory air of the springtime trek, fall migration instead smacks of self-fulfillment, the aftereffects of difficult tasks now laid behind. In numbers swollen with youngsters, mutually congratulatory Robins parade southward in a cheery epilogue to their prolific propagative achievements.

As was characteristic of the spring trip, fall migration is a most discontinuous event. Much of this discontinuity arises from regional variations in temperature (since warmspells induce northward retracings) as well as in food supplies (since local abundancies stall the migration, while scarcities hasten it). Though normally traveling at such modest rates as twenty to thirty miles daily, Robins may scramble one hundred fifty miles in a single day if, having been lulled behind schedule by cozy temperatures or abundant berries, they suddenly get nipped in their posteriors by a scolding Jack Frost.

Although, loosely speaking, Robins fly south in the fall, they do not actually follow a strictly southern course most of the time. Birds who are migrating in the eastern portion of the continent, for example, fly in a decidedly southwesterly direction—and with good reason, since a purely southward flight would carry them out over the Atlantic Ocean. (This is not to say that Robins simply follow the coastline, however, since birds who are well inland pursue a southwesterly direction too.) In complementary fashion, Redbreasts in the western part of the continent tend, with some exception, to follow southeasterly courses.

Where exactly in the South do migrating Robins go? The vast majority—some 80 percent—fly to the Gulf states, and many of the remaining birds go to the coastal areas between North Carolina and Florida where the ocean acts to moderate winter weather. A small percentage may go into Mexico—Robins have been found as far south as Pachuca, Hildalgo, which is about seven hundred miles below San Antonio, Texas—but most Redbreasts remain in the United States. Mexico, no doubt, is usually too warm for Robins, who seem to prefer winter temperatures between 40°F and 60°F.

In any event, the specific southern region to which a given Robin migrates depends in part upon the longitudinal location of that bird's breeding grounds. Most Robins who summered in eastern North America migrate to the region lying between Florida and Louisiana; those who summered in the Far West generally head for the Texas-to-Louisiana region; and those who bred in the central part of the continent may end up anywhere from Florida to Texas. In other words, although there is a wide range of potential wintering homes for any given group of Robins, no westerners vacation in Florida and no easterners fly to Texas.

Surprisingly, not all of the Robins within a given breeding locality migrate to the same place. To borrow an example provided by one ornithologist, a Redbreast from Chicago may head to Miami while his next-door neighbor may fly instead to Houston. Thus, rather than all Robins from a given area migrating together to a specific southern resort, the birds instead migrate "in a random manner, so that Robins that summered in a given locality scatter widely in the Winter" (Speirs, 1946). Robins still migrate in flocks, of course, but each flock may contain representatives of many different breeding localities rather than just one.

One striking aspect of fall migration—a characteristic which is not shared by the springtime journey—is the great degree to which many humans care about the Robin's ability to make the trip. Should a Robin become injured during his stay in the South and for that reason be unable to fly back to his breeding grounds in the spring, no one is likely to give the problem much thought. But let a bird be unable to fly south in the fall so that he is seemingly at winter's mercy, and he will be whisked off to Florida like some foreign dignitary on a matter of utmost importance. One Robin, for example, was felled by a stone just as winter arrived at Racine, Wisconsin. This poor fellow was half-frozen when rescued by the Racine police, who patiently nursed him back to health. Headache gone and blood de-iced, the reprieved Redbreast was then rushed to Jacksonville, Florida, aboard a southbound train.

Then there was the case of "Joe," a Robin who was stranded in chilly upstate New York (Malone, to be exact) after being grounded by an untimely cat-attack. Suffering from a broken wing, Joe wisely let himself be captured by a sweethearted florist who paid a special bird-rate of $6.63 for a one-way plane ticket to Miami. More than three hundred people gathered to wish Joe *bon voyage* as he began his first-class Eastern Airlines flight to the sunshine state. Smug with the knowledge that he had just set a tough-to-beat Robin record for the fastest migration time, Joe quickly recovered from his injury and was soon released to bask in palm trees and romp in the surf. Presumably, Joe flew the thirteen-hundred-mile return trip under his own power with fellow Redbreasts the following spring.

Implicit in such anecdotes, of course, is the presumption that migration comprises a difficult journey that is manageable only by the fully fit. No doubt migration is indeed a hardship, for many birds die along the way. Yet through fate or providence, some blatantly handicapped misfits occasionally manage to negotiate the long trip quite successfully. One such miracle involved a male whose body was pierced by a stick which

> appeared to enter the back at the left of the backbone and behind the heart and the lungs, penetrating the body in the area of the stomach and kidneys, but just enough to one side to miss them. . . . About two inches of the stick projected from the back of the bird, and about an inch protruded from the breast. (Nichols, 1944)

In 1941, this sorrily shish-kabobbed soul—presumably the victim of some accidental impalement—mated and reared two broods of young in Saddle River, New Jersey. He then disappeared for two years but reappeared in 1943 on the same lawn as before, and still sporting the unwieldy stick. Conceivably, this plucky bird was among the handful of Robins who, as we're about to see, remain North in the winter; much more likely, however, he not only migrated south with fellow Redbreasts but made the round trip twice to boot.

Winter

Although nearly all north-breeding Robins migrate south in the fall, a small but reliable core of foolhardy heroes inevitably chooses to defy winter's icy onslaughts by remaining far above the Mason-Dixon line. Before we consider the 98 percent of the Robin population that does migrate, let's first take a look at the nonconformists—those Winter Robins of the North.

Winter Robins

Robins of both sexes can be found throughout winter in regions as far north as upper Newfoundland and British Columbia. Since these birds are usually both few in number and hidden within heavily wooded areas, they are seldom noticed by people.

However, one winter in downtown Ottawa, Ontario, several Robins "took up headquarters in trees around Parliament, where their well-known call notes greeted passersby and made them wonder whether the seasons had suddenly been shifted" (Eifrig, 1910).

One popular explanation of Winter Robins holds that the birds actually migrate from breeding grounds that are farther north than their winter locations. Winter Robins in New England, for example, are commonly presumed to be native Newfoundlanders who migrated only as far south as New England before prematurely settling down (Winter Robins in New Jersey, meanwhile, are presumed to be birds who had bred in New England, and so on). In other words, Winter Robins are often thought to represent a process of mini-migration, whereby the summer residents of a given locality are replaced by birds from areas slightly farther north. This mini-migration theory, by the way, usually presupposes that Robins who breed in the Far North are "hardier" than those who summer at lower latitudes. Thus Canadian Robins are often believed to be more vigorous and cold-resistant than New England Robins, and that is the supposed reason why the Canadians are able to withstand New England winters while the New Englanders move to the milder South.

As plausible as this theory sounds, mini-migration seems to account for only a small minority of Winter Robins. Instead, the majority are in fact the same birds who bred at the localities wherein they now winter (thus Winter Robins in New England are not usually summer residents of Canada, but are native New Englanders). There is, furthermore, no reason whatsoever to think that northern Robins are inherently more hardy than any of their southern relatives. Unfortunately, at present there seems to be no satisfactory explanation of why some Robins ignore, or fail to possess, normal impulses to migrate south in the fall.

Regardless of their origins, Winter Robins in any event face numerous problems of survival, the foremost being the procurement of sufficient food. Naturally, adequate shelter from the biting wind is also important, but satisfactory cover can usually be obtained fairly readily from evergreen groves and thicketed swamps. Warmth, in and of itself, comprises a less essential need since Robins seem quite able to cope with extremely low temperatures so long as the birds are well fed; indeed, in some Canadian regions, Robins have displayed no distress nor even discomfort despite refrigeratory temperatures as low as 30° or 40° below zero! Food, then, not warmth, is the *sine qua non* of the Robin's survival in the wintery north.

Freezing temperatures, of course, can render once-juicy berries into unpalatably petrified pebbles. Nevertheless, Winter Robins cannot afford to be finicky, and the birds generally eat anything they can find. The berries of sumac and mountain ash are common mainstays in the North, but nearly any fruit—including such autumn leftovers as frozen apples and pears—is patiently chiseled away. Sometimes the birds can supplement their impoverished diet with tasty worms during rare midwinter warmspells or, perhaps, near a bubbly hot spring that thaws the surrounding ground. Robins who winter near the coast can even occasionally add seafood to their diets; in one account, Redbreasts near Godbout, Quebec, gathered on the low-tide shores of the St. Lawrence to scavenge such fare as whelks and seaweed amid broken chunks of ice. Despite all of these chance sources of nutrition, however, food in the wintery North is seldom reliable or extensive enough to support Robins in any great number. Only as individuals scattered here and there can the birds find sufficient provisions to last until the affluence of spring returns.

Even when a single Robin has an entire berry patch to himself, starvation may nevertheless threaten long before winter has run its course. Indeed, an attractive fruitpatch found in the fall may in fact prove lethal by luring a Redbreast away from its migratory inclinations. Once cold weather has arrived, the Robin will be largely committed to remaining at the fruitpatch because scouting for food in the relative barren of surrounding areas would require more energy than the bird can now afford on its winter rations. Even if the fruitpatch later becomes dangerously depleted, the Robin will probably stay there because the patch

> is still likely to be the best spot within the reduced explorable area available to the Robin, with its reduced energy resources. As the days get shorter and colder, more and more of the Robin's energy must be used up merely staying warm and alive, so less and less will be available for the luxury of exploring. Thus the food patch may act as a trap for southbound Robins, and if the supply is not large enough to last through the winter, it may be a fatal trap. (Aldrich, 1945)

Once Robins have become significantly undernourished, their demise can occur in any number of unpleasant ways. Numbed by cold and weakened with hunger, they may slowly succumb to the elements if not to outright starvation; alternatively, the sluggish birds may perish more quickly under the slashing talons of a swooping owl or the crunching jaws of a pouncing cat.

Incidentally, the fact that those Robins who do have sufficient food are able to endure northern winters implies that the southward exodus of the general population is necessitated by lack of food in the bleak North, and not by lack of warmth. This in turn suggests more generally that the migratory habits of a given avian species (for example, Robins) do not necessarily reflect climatic frailty compared to those nonmigratory species (such as Mockingbirds) which hold year-round residence in the North. It is probably the ability to find food during winter—rather than the ability to withstand cold—that usually separates migratory from nonmigratory species.

What can you do to help the Winter Robins in your locality? Not being seed-eaters and seldom accepting suet, Robins will not

profit from the normal foodfare that people usually offer birds in winter, although Redbreasts will eat bread crumbs occasionally. Blueberries and most other small fruits are normally as unavailable to humans as to Robins during the winter months, but with proper foresight such Robin delights can be frozen and stored during the fall. On the other hand, raisins, olives, and apples (served baked or raw) can be bought year-round, and most Robins will dine on these with heart-warmed thanks. Redbreasts will also occasionally eat cottage cheese, corn biscuits, and sometimes even cooked spaghetti. All of these items may be more readily accepted if placed out on the ground rather than on a birdfeeder.

Robins in the South

While Winter Robins are fighting cold and hunger in the North, most of their kinsmen are enjoying relatively mild and bounteous conditions in the South. Initially feasting within berry-laden woodlands, the birds eventually strip every tree and bush of its fruit and so shift, in late winter, to parks, fields, and similar areas to hunt ground-living insects. Throughout their stay in the South, Robins retain much the same personality they displayed during.fall; in short, they are extremely wary of people, they are nonterritorial and gather in great flocks, and they wander about the countryside almost continuously.

Years ago, the extreme shyness of Robins was intensified by bird-hunting southerners who, for reasons discussed earlier, have in the past relished Redbreasts more with their palates than with their hearts. As recently as the 1920s, such killing—although by then illegal—still persisted in certain areas. Relating this situation to the Robin's wintery shyness, one writer from Biloxi, Mississippi, remarked:

> The Robin here is by no means the bird of lawns and garden as in the north in summer, but is as wild as the wildest and frequents only remote districts for

feeding and roosting here in winter. Perhaps the fact that Robin-pie is still considered a delicacy by Negroes and "poor whites" is partly responsible for this condition. (Corrington, 1922)

Even though nowadays Robins are no longer hunted, they remain shy creatures in winter, for shyness is part and parcel of their nonbreeding personality.

The flocks that Robins form in wintertime are usually quite large, often numbering fifty thousand or more; one aggregation of Western Robins in Oakland, California, was estimated at one hundred sixty-five thousand birds, and even larger flocks are sometimes reported. In those localities where they happen to congregate, Robins virtually dominate the countryside, as indicated in the following report from Hancock County, Mississippi:

Over great tracts of young pine, cleared land, and burnt forest, we often walked, seeing hardly any birds but these [Robins]. They flushed before us at almost every step and soon became an important feature of the landscape. (Allison, 1906)

Robins so utterly ubiquitous that they flush "at almost every step"? Surely such a thought strains the imagination of us northerners who are so accustomed to seeing Redbreasts scattered in mere two's and three's about our lawns!

The Robin's great flocks—so impressive in size—are all the more striking when they are on the move, which often they are. Some of their incessant wandering is prompted by food—more particularly, the availability of such berries as palmetto, hackberry, sour gum, holly, chinaberry, cedarberries, hawthorne, and mistletoe—for the simple reason that the Robin's huge flocks will soon deplete a fruitpatch of almost any size. Thus the birds move largely in quest of continuing sustenance.

Temperature, however, also guides the winter wanderings of Redbreasts, and does so in much the same way as during fall migration. More specifically, one researcher who studied the winter movements of Robins in the South found that

> during periods when temperatures were falling sharply or were continually cold, the trend of the movements [of Robins] was southward; when the temperatures were rising sharply and were continuously warm, the trend of the movements was northward. In other words, the Robins continued to move during the Winter in much the same manner as during the Autumn, except that during the Autumn, periods of falling temperature predominated so that there was a final resultant shift to the south. (Speirs, 1946)

Thus it appears that—at least so far as the effects of temperature are concerned—the winter movements of Robins are fundamentally similar to the birds' movements during fall migration. As you will recall, in fact, Redbreasts move precisely the same way during spring migration as well (they head northward during warm weather and southward during cold). In short, the fall, winter, and spring movements of Robins do not represent discrete phases in the species' life cycle, but rather reflect a single response pattern to changing thermostimulation.

In any event, the winter wanderings of flocking Robins frequently result in sudden, massive invasions of southern districts which only a short while earlier had been completely devoid of Redbreasts. Occasionally the birds even march into urban areas, especially if these places happen to be rich in foodstuff. For days or even weeks, ten thousand Robins may occupy a city before finally departing just as suddenly as they had arrived, and leaving the town Robinless once more.

For all their great mobility, however, Robins may become entrapped by a snowstorm even in the Deep South during unusually severe winters. If harsh enough, these storms can kill, not through cold but by putting all food supplies under wraps. Many years ago, for example, an especially bad storm in St.

Petersburg, Florida, killed Robins by the thousands. Although city residents tried to feed the birds soaked bread,

> there was such a shortage of food generally that [people] swept up and hauled out truckloads of dead Robins from the parks and streets of St. Petersburg; upon dissection, they were found to be empty of all signs of food, literally starved to death. (Quoted by Speirs, 1946)

Like an army amassed within a small space, the Robin population is most vulnerable to wholesale destruction during those winter months when the bulk of its members are stationed within the relatively limited area of the Gulf states. And, like an overpowering enemy that in one great stroke deals a crippling blow to its opponent, a single winter storm may inflict so many casualties upon Robins in the South that their ranks will be noticeably thinned throughout the year to come.

chapter 12

Robins and People

I went down through the garden calling softly, "Bobby, Bobby," but there was no reply. . . . Then a search was made. Under the grapevine was found his body, the breast torn and bloody, shot by an air-rifle at close range. Bobby was undoubtedly waiting under the grape-arbor for his breakfast, and when a boy approached with his rifle, he just thought it was another kind human to feed him. And so he faced the boy confidently and trustingly and received the cruel shot in his breast.

That little lame Robin taught me many lovely things that I could not have learned in any other way. He taught me that our Robins have a high degree of intelligence, that they are perfectly capable of learning new things. He taught me that the fear of human beings is not instinctive but is taught them by the parent birds. He taught me that our wild birds are capable of love, trust, and devotion. I taught him only one thing: that was to love and trust human beings, and that was his undoing.

—A.F. Gardner, 1934

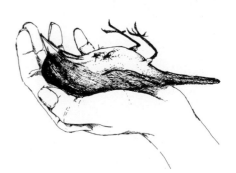

In describing the life cycle of the American Robin, we have noted many points of intersection with the lifeways of humans.

Some of these junctions have been characterized by great injury, for we have slaughtered Robins in southern roosts, poisoned them with pernicious pesticides, and blasted them with thundering shotguns. But there have been benevolent interactions as well. Early colonists fondly christened Robins after their beloved English bird; homeowners welcome Robins as nesting neighbors and adopt helpless nestlings when circumstances demand; human passersby often aid troubled Robins who are entangled with string, undernourished during a snowy winter, or stranded north in the fall.

In short, people are sometimes the Robin's enemy and sometimes his friend. And whatever that truism may lack in profundity is, I'm afraid, more than compensated by immutability. And yet, pause for a moment. Does contemplation of our double-edged relationship with Robins really lack profundity, or does it simply seem to because it is so obvious? There is , I believe, something deeply important to be inferred from the marked antithesis that frequently exists in human values—values such as those experienced by Bobby, a little lame Robin who lived in the hands of human compassion and died at the hands of human callosity.

Other thoughts, perhaps, could be derived from our survey of *Turdus migratorius,* but two Robins are tapping at my window now, and I've never been able to resist their invitations.

References

Aldrich, John W. Additional breeding and migration records of the Black-Backed Robin. *Auk,* 1945, 62: 310-311.

Allison, Andrew. Notes on winter birds of Hancock County, Mississippi. *Auk,* 1906, 23: 47.

Amadon, Dean. Migratory birds of relict distribution. *Auk,* 1953, 70: 464.

Ardrey, Robert. *The Territorial Imperative.* New York: Dell Publishing Co., 1966.

Audubon, John James. *The Birds of America.* New York: V.G. Audubon, 1856.

Bird uses worm as lure. *The New York Times,* 5 August 1934, IV, 7:1.

Caras, Roger. *Source of the Thunder.* New York: Popular Library, 1970.

Corrington, Julian D. Winter birds of the Biloxi, Mississippi, region. *Auk,* 1922, 39: 554.

Eifrig, G. A winter of rare birds at Ottawa, Ontario. *Auk,* 1910, 27: 58.

Etter, A.G. When a state spray kills the state bird: Michigan's Robin Redbreast. *Audubon Magazine,* 1963, 65: 134-137.

Fireman frees tangled Robin. *The New York Times*, 25 April 1934, 2:2.

Forbush, Edward Howe. *Birds of Massachusetts and Other New England States*. Norwood, Mass.: Norwood Press, J.S. Cushing Co., 1929.

Gardner, A.F. Bringing up a Robin. *Bird-Lore*, 1934, 36: 174-175.

George, J. Here come the Robins! *Reader's Digest*, 1964, 84: 217-220.

Halle, Louis J., Jr. Habits of the American Robin. In *Audubon Nature Encyclopedia* (Vol. 9). New York: Curtis Publishing Co., 1965.

Heppner, F. Science proves it: The Robin sees the worm. *Audubon Magazine*, 1967, 69: 86-88.

Hickey, Joseph J. *A Guide to Bird Watching*. New York: Oxford University Press, 1943.

Howe, Reginald Heber. Breeding habits of the American Robin in eastern Massachusetts. *Auk*, 1898, 15: 162-167.

Mackay, George H. A great flight of Robins in Florida. *Auk*, 1897, 14: 325.

Melvin, A. Gordon. Robin in the kitchen. *Hobbies*, 1962, 67: 130.

Merriam, Florence A. *Birds of Village and Field*. Boston: Houghton, Mifflin & Co., 1898.

Miller, Olive Thorne. The Robin. *Atlantic Monthly*, 1883, 52: 644.

Nice, Margaret M. Robins and Carolina Chickadees remating. *Bird-Banding*, 1933, 4: 157.

Nichols, C.K. Peculiar injury to a Robin. *Auk*, 1944, 61: 466-467.

Parsons, Katharine S. Our Robin's nest. *Bird-Lore*, 1906, 8: 66-67.

Pearson, T. Gilbert (ed.). Wanted—A patron for a million Robins. *Bird-Lore*, 1931, 33: 221-223.

Pettingill, Olin Sewall, Jr. *Ornithology in Laboratory and Field.* Minneapolis, Minn.: Burgess Publishing Co., 1970.

Porter, Gene. *What I Have Done With Birds.* Indianapolis: Bobbs-Merrill Co., 1907.

Speirs, J.M. Local and migratory movements of the American Robin in eastern North America. Unpublished doctoral dissertation, University of Illinois, 1946.

Torrey, B. Robin roosts. *Atlantic Monthly,* 1890, 66: 492-498.

Trenary, D.C. That cheerful songster, the Robin. *Science Digest,* 1954, 35(4): 7-10.

Tyler, Winsor Marrett. In *Life Histories of North American Thrushes, Kinglets, and Their Allies,* ed. by Arthur Cleveland Bent. Washington, D.C.: Smithsonian Institution, U.S. National Museum Bulletin 196, 1949.

Wallace, G.J. Are our songbirds doomed? *Science Digest,* 1959, 45(6): 43-47.

Weeks, Leroy Titus. Who builds the nest? *Bird-Lore,* 1923, 25: 254-255.

Wilson, Etta S. Strange conduct of a Robin. *Auk,* 1919, 36: 584.

Young, Howard. Atypical copulatory behavior of a Robin. *Auk,* 1949, 66: 94.

Index